KREWE

KREWE

THE EARLY NEW ORLEANS CARNIVAL
COMUS TO ZULU

CARNIVAL
PRESS

ERROL LABORDE

2007
CARNIVAL PRESS

ISBN-13: 978-0-9792273-0-1
ISBN-10: 0-9792273-0-5

CARNIVAL PRESS
110 Veterans Blvd. Suite 123
Metairie, La. 70005
(504) 830-7235

HALF-TITLE PAGE: *Formation Area of the First Rex Parade, 1872.* The
*parade began at the Clay statue which stood on Canal Street at Royal
Street. This detail of a George Schmidt painting originally appeared as
a proclamation poster for the Rex organization.* GEORGE SCHMIDT

FACING TITLE PAGE: *Twelfth Night Revelers Ball illustration detail,
ca. 1873. Founded in 1870, the group paraded through 1876. TNR's
ball is still staged in celebration of each Twelfth Night.*
THE HISTORIC NEW ORLEANS COLLECTION
1975.117.10

COVER AND HALF-TITLE PAGE IMAGES: by George Schmidt.
Thanks to Mr. Schmidt and the Rex School of Design

Printed in Canada by Friesens Book Division

MARCHING ORDER

PREFACE

FATE HAD MADE JULIA STREET my home base during the Carnival season of 2006. Like a million other people who had post-Katrina stories to tell, my story was that we stayed in a small apartment at 604 Julia for five months while our Mid-City home was being restored.

At a time when Katrina had made just about every facet of life different in New Orleans, so too had Carnival been effected. City Hall had demanded that the parade schedule be reduced. Some of the krewes that did march barely had the resources to stage a parade, so their processions were scaled down; other krewes, particularly the big names, maintained their size. Just about all the parades were united in poking fun at the frustration we were all experiencing.

Some people argued that the parades should not be held at all, but reason prevailed. Instead of the world getting a message that New Orleans was too battered to even stage its Carnival, it saw instead a city recovering and that still had its spirit. Carnival 2006 was the first big event in the city after Katrina and did much to help New Orleanians believe in themselves. Never has a Mardi Gras celebration meant so much.

Julia Street proved to be a great place for parade watching. From our apartment we only had to walk down the block to the corner of Julia and St. Charles where all the parades passed. Vendor trucks stationed at the corners provided sterling renditions of parade cuisines, particularly polish sausage on a bun and corn dogs.

More than just a good vantage point, Julia Street is hallowed ground in the history of the New Orleans Carnival. Two blocks toward the Mississippi River from where we watched the parades is the corner of Julia and Magazine Streets. It was from that corner on February 24, 1857 that the Mistick Krewe of Comus began its first parade. Moving toward St. Charles the parade was a visual spectacle in those days before bead throwing when such processions were to be viewed and admired.

There had been Carnival-related parades in New Orleans before Comus, but nothing that lasted. During Comus' first 150 years (1857-2007) it would set the template for all else to follow,

History tends to become easily muddled, sanctifying half-truths and relying on untested anecdotes. Something as carefree as Carnival celebrations are particularly vulnerable to historic misinterpretation because they often escape close examination. Yet to understand Carnival is to understand elements of politics, social standing, religion, customs and community "do-gooderism."

This book looks at the first sixty years from that first Comus parade with the hope of presenting new facts and reinterpreting some lore that had been accepted as factual. The period, which stretched to the founding of the Zulu organization, was a fascinating time in which the city suffered through the Civil War and tried to rebuild itself. Carnival, more than anyone realized, was a tool in that rebuilding.

I was blessed to be on Julia Street during the Carnival of 2006 although for the most tragic of reasons. As the New Orleans Carnival approached its 150th anniversary I could hear the drums echo off the same buildings from which they did a century and a half ago. There could be no better setting for going back to the beginning.

—ERROL LABORDE

ACKNOWLEDGMENTS

I HAVE NEVER KNOWN a Krewe Captain to say that he could put his event together all alone; the same goes for book authors. There are many to whom I owe appreciation:

To the Rex School of Design, particularly John Charbonnet, William Grace, Jonathan McCall and Philip Woollam. Their decision to hire me to author the Rex 125th anniversary book, *Marched the Day God* created breakthrough research opportunities. Some of the chapters in this book are based on sections from the Rex publication, all containing new information that was not available at the time.

To the owners of New Orleans Magazine: MC Media and then Renaissance Publishing Company. Sections of this book are based on research from that publication.

To Mary Lou Eichhorn and Doris Ann Gorman, researchers extraordinary. Their sleuthing helped lead to many key discoveries.

To those who provided the art, particularly Arthur Nead the gifted artist who illustrated the book's essay section and who has for many years created images for my Streetcar column, first in *Gambit* and then in *New Orleans Magazine*. Special thanks to John Magill of the Historic New Orleans Collection for his help and expertise in gathering early photographic images and to the Collection for the great service it provides. And of course to George Schmidt whose painting graces this cover. His skill and his passion for historic art qualify him as a local treasure.

To Michael Ledet for his keen eye in designing this book and to Patricia Brady for her insights and advice about publishing.

To all the Krewe Captains and members. They continue to give the city a valuable, and underappreciated, gift.

And most of all—to my wife Peggy Scott Laborde. This project was nearly a victim of the Katrina intrusion. Her encouragement kept the project alive, her enthusiasm and support made it worthwhile. This book is dedicated to her.

Formation Area of the First Rex Parade, 1872. *The parade began·at the Clay statue which stood on Canal Street at Royal Street. King Lewis Salomon is on horseback wearing a borrowed costume from a local production of "Richard III." Riders are masked as Bedouins. This detail of a George Schmidt painting originally appeared as a proclamation poster for the Rex organization.* GEORGE SCHMIDT

Illustration detail of second Comus parade, 1858. *Whereas the krewe's premier parade the previous year only had two floats, the '58 march featured thirty "tableaux roulants" and became the model for all New Orleans Carnival parades to come.*

1

WHO WERE THOSE GUYS?
COMUS AND THE MEN WHO MADE MARDI GRAS

THROUGHOUT THE VIEUX CARRE shoppers and workers headed home on this Winter Saturday evening while others arrived for their night out. From the east came the sounds of the port, the panting of steam engines and the songs of a calliope. The street itself was loud with the clatter of horse-drawn carriages and the echoes off the aged buildings. Smells of Creole dishes wafted from various kitchens. At one such place, the Gem Cafe on Royal Street, the evening was going to be especially busy. Upstairs some men were meeting to form a secret club as men of that day commonly did. No woman sipping from her demitasse in the Gem's dining room, no man puffing on his cigar, could know that the night, January 10, 1857 would be one of those moments caressed by posterity. Within the universe of New Orleans culture and the evolution of the American carnival, the world would change that evening. Memories of the Gem and the men who gathered upstairs would be preserved. As though the sounds from the street created a symphony of drums, the pageantry was about to begin.

In late 1856 a group of men had been having informal talks at Pope's Pharmacy, located on the corner of Jackson Avenue and Prytania Street.

Tradition has usually described these men as being from Mobile, Alabama and not at all pleased with the lack of decorum in the New Orleans Carnival. Hoping to bring a bit of Mobilian creativity to their new hometown, they decided to form a carnival group. On January 3, 1857 an invitation signed by the six men was sent to selected friends. The invitation was simply worded, but those words would reverberate, in New Orleans at least, through the ages:

"You are requested to meet a few of your friends at the Club room over the Gem, on Royal Street, on Saturday, 10th, at 7 o'clock."

Signing the invitation, in this order, were the six men who had met at Pope's Pharmacy: S.M. Todd, L.D. Addison, J.H. Pope, Frank Shaw, Jr., Joseph Ellison and William P. Ellison. In his classic study of the New Orleans Carnival's origins, *The Mistick Krewe: Chronicles of Comus and His Kin* author Perry Young described Joseph Ellison as being the "moving spirit."

At the appointed hour of January 10, thirteen men responded to the invitation and met with the original six at the Gem, a popular cafe located on the 100 block of Royal Street. Among the new thirteen was Charles M. Churchill, a local hardware merchant who would become one of the major figures in the organization that was to evolve.

A second meeting was held at the Gem on February 8. By this time the membership had grown to fifty-eight. Following the suggestion of Pope, at whose apothecary the original meeting was held, the group would be known as The Mistick Krewe of Comus.

Comus would change everything about the New Orleans Carnival and the way it was celebrated. Prior to the Mistick Krewe there were miscellaneous celebrations in the city, including a New Orleans version of Mobile's Cowbellions Society, but nothing that lasted. Comus would define the New Orleans style of parade, establish the word "krewe," and mix in heavy doses of secrecy and tradition. All else that would follow, from Alla to Zulu, was shaped by Comus. Prior to Comus, Carnival in New Orleans would stagger and stop, but once Comus began, the New Orleans Carnival, as though suddenly nurtured by elixir from Dr. Pope's Pharmacy, would grow and become strong.

Eighty-three men took part in the first Comus parade on February 24, 1857. Not included was an aspiring businessman named

A.W. Merriam who was one of thirty-eight new members admitted after the initial parade.

Merriam, along with Churchill and the original six, would become pivotal figures in the evolution of the New Orleans Carnival. A festival as big and as all-encompassing as Mardi Gras is the product of many minds, but all things begin with those who had the original ideas and who established the precedents that the future would follow. Those eight are the ones described here as "The Men Who Made Mardi Gras."

Though the original six are often thought of as being from Mobile, only three, the Ellison brothers and Todd, lived there at some point in their lives. though none was a native of that town. Most of the eight were Yankees whose activities would transport the New Orleans Carnival from being strictly a French Creole festival to something that would become distinctively American. The Mardi Gras parading traditions transported from Mobile were probably more a product of the nation's melting pot than the French skillet.

Northerners looking for opportunity in the South likely carried with them the Mummers tradition of masquerade marches and New Year's parades developed in the ethnic neighborhoods of Philadelphia. At each stop the method of celebration would be reworked, finally reaching New Orleans where the French term "Mardi Gras" would be applied to what would become the ultimate American Carnival. For that to happen though required the imagination and good works of these eight men:

JOHN H. POPE

An obviously literate man, Pope had a good enough grasp of Greek and Roman mythology to suggest the Comus name. Pope's Pharmacy was a popular gathering spot of the day. He also lived in the building. Many early members of Comus came from that uptown neighborhood.

Like all of the founders of the Mistick Krewe, Pope, who was 30 at the time of the first meeting, was a young man. He was born in Brooklyn, New York in 1827. We know he was living in New Orleans by 1850 because by that year he is listed as a medical clerk for the federal government with an office at 128 Camp Street. He also married in New Orleans, to Renette Willard Childs in 1853.

Later in 1857 the men who founded Comus also formed a luncheon club known as the Pickwick Club. Until 1888, membership in the Pickwick Club and Comus were the same, though a member was allowed to acknowledge his membership in the former but never the latter. As a founder of Comus, Pope was also a founder of the Pickwick though there is some confusion about his roles in each. A 1964 book about the organization, *The Pickwick Club of New Orleans* by Augusto P. Miceli, states flatly that on "February 15, 1857, John H. Pope was unanimously elected captain of the Krewe." Later in the book, Charles Churchill is listed as the Pickwick Club's first president and Pope as "Captain General of the Krewe." All other knowledgeable publications however, including a centennial book published by Comus in 1957, list Churchill as the first captain.

Either way, Pope was a major influence in the founding of both organizations. Pope died in 1887 and was buried in New Orleans at St. Joseph Cemetery. That's significant because St. Joseph's is a Catholic cemetery. Comus represented the Anglo-Saxon invasion of a French-Catholic celebration. Pope may have been the only Roman Catholic among the founders.

Miceli says of Pope that he was "one of the most respected and influential members of the original group. His apothecary shop at the corner of Jackson Avenue and Prytania Street was a favorite meeting place for the young men of the neighborhood." During those gatherings the germination of an idea began that would become Comus.

JOSEPH ELLISON AND WILLIAM P. ELLISON

Seven years separated these two brothers. In 1857 Joseph was 32 and William was 39. The younger was born in Louisville, the other in Pittsburgh. In New Orleans, both lived at the corner of what is now St. Charles Avenue and Second Street. At the time William was listed as a cotton broker with the firm of Ellison and Coste; Joseph was a 'commission merchant' with the firm of Pope, Ellison and Co., a name that suggests some connection with the family of fellow-founder John Pope.

Joseph Ellison could very well be THE person who got the New Orleans Carnival celebration as we would know it started. He seemed to be in charge at that first meeting at the Gem Cafe announcing, according to Miceli, that the purpose of the meeting was "the formation of an association similar to the Cowbellians of Mobile." At that meeting Joseph was elected vice-president of the fledgling krewe with Churchill as president. Joseph would eventually serve two stints as captain, 1858–59 and 1866–71.

In February 1955, the *Times-Picayune* published an interview with Joseph's then 91-year-old daughter, Emilie Ellison, who had been invited to attend the Comus Ball that year. In the article, entitled, "Comus Founder's Life Is Recalled," Emilie Ellison remembered her father as a "very affable redheaded man." She revealed that during the Civil War her father had traveled north to raise money for the southern cause. While on his journey, he was arrested, charged with espionage and sent to prison on the Dry Tortuga Islands off the Florida coast. The *Picayune* article described Joseph as being the "first Comus captain," bringing to three, along with Pope and Churchill, the number of people about whom that claim was made. He was clearly at least the second Comus captain. Was the daughter impressed with her father as captain? "He just looked like papa to me," she answered.

Both brothers spent time growing up in Mobile, where they became familiar with the Cowbellians. There they married sisters from a Pascagoula, Mississippi French family; Joseph to Hermina Delmas, William to Marie Henriette Delmas.

William seems to have been less active than his younger brother in the formative stages though he is listed as a founder of the Pickwick Club. His will suggested some family discord and concern about succession laws though he did speak fondly of Joseph who he credited with having helped him amass "fortunes well in excess of their rela-

tives." Joseph's greatest sacrifice for his brother came in 1877 when he
went to visit William who was dying from smallpox. While there,
Joseph contracted the disease as well and died four days after William.
The two were buried at the Old Spanish Fort Cemetery in Pascagoula.
The cemetery was heavily damaged in 1998 by Hurricane Georges,
and the Ellison tombs were apparently among those destroyed. Once
again, the Ellison Brothers faced an ending together.

SAMUEL MANNING TODD

Here was a man who—quite literally—gave Comus much of its early
color. At the time of the krewe's founding, his business was "S.D.M.
Todd & Co., Paints and Varnishes" located at 90 Magazine Street. A
year later a newspaper advertisement described the company as "deal-
ers in Artists' Fine Colors and Tools. And Painters' materials of every
description."

Another Yankee in this saga, Todd was born in Utica, New York
in 1815, making him at 42 the oldest of the founders. He had originally moved to New Orleans in the 1830s and then relocated in
Mobile where his brothers lived. There he proved be quite adept at
politics. An accountant by trade, he was elected that town's city treasurer and then later its comptroller. In Mobile Todd would have
moved in the right circles so that he could have been active in the
Cowbellians and other carnival groups. An older brother, John B.
Todd, was a prominent artist in Mobile. John's obituary in 1866 credited him with being largely responsible for making the Cowbellians
more respectable. John appears to have been a major influence on his
younger brother in terms of professional and social connections.
Samuel probably had much to do with transporting the Cowbellians
tradition to New Orleans.

In 1854 Samuel Todd moved back in New Orleans where he
opened his paint business and became active in the military. His real
mark in life, however, was with another mystic crew—the Masons.
At the time of his death in 1905 he was listed as Louisiana's oldest
past grand master. A monument to him in the Masonic Cemetery on

City Park Avenue in New Orleans described him as a "distinguished citizen and free mason."

Masonry and other secretive men's organization were quite popular in the mid 19th century. In Mobile secret societies were so prevalent that the town would be referred to as "The Mother of Mystics." Todd's association with such organizations may have influenced the good-natured secretiveness that Comus introduced to New Orleans carnival organizations. More than anyone else he could have been the one to enforce the mystic in the Mistick Krewe.

FRANKLIN SHAW, JR.

While Todd was the oldest of the founders, Shaw (28) was the youngest. He too was a New Yorker born in New York City. In 1857 he was operating Frank Shaw, Jr. & Co. , produce and commission merchants, located at 80 Tchoupitoulas Street. Like all of the Comus founders he is also listed as a Pickwick Club founder. Shaw, who was elected to be the first treasurer of the new krewe, is representative of the young male merchant class that typified Comus membership.

Something else that typified the founders would be service in the upcoming Civil War. At age 35 he would enlist as a private in the Washington Artillery, an elite Louisiana unit of the Confederate Army.

Service in the Confederacy is often misunderstood in terms of modern political interpretation. At the time there was not the sense of an indivisible nation promoted by Abraham Lincoln. Though many of the professional young men of that day were from the north, the south was where they saw their destiny and economic opportunity. For men who lived in the city there were many reasons, apart from the slavery issue, to join the Confederate army including the reality that everyone else was doing it, and that, in the long run, doing so could be good for business. There was also the perceived excitement of being part of building a new nation.

At the time of the Comus founding Shaw was living at 275 Magazine Street in what is now the Warehouse District—a setting where many young businessmen would meet and talk. In these peaceful years before the War, forming a carnival krewe was also something that, among his peers, everyone was doing.

L.D. ADDISON

Much of what we know about the initial meetings of Comus may be because of Lloyd Dulaney Addison, Jr. Among the initial temporary officers, he was elected secretary. All of the original six served on various committees and were among the founders of the Pickwick Club.

At 29, Addison was the second youngest of the founders. As is true of all the other founders he was a native of neither New Orleans nor Mobile. Addison was born in Kentucky to parents who were originally from Maryland. At the time of Comus' founding he lived on Dauphine Street near Canal Street and was associated with the firm of Ross, Addison and Co., described as commission merchants of sugar and molasses. All of the original six were given the responsibility to "introduce such persons as they might deem worthy of being members of this association." Among those that Addison likely deemed worthy was his business partner, 26-year-old E.M. Ross, who is listed among the founders of the Pickwick and was among those invited to the meeting at the Gem Cafe. The six founders not only set a new direction for Carnival, they drew the original participants from their friends and co-workers.

CHARLES H. CHURCHILL

Here was a man who was a fast climber. Charles Holliday Churchill was not among those who met at Pope's Pharmacy, but was among the 13 invited guests who met at the Gem. Before the evening was over, Churchill was elected to be the group's president. In June, 1857 when a social wing of Comus was created in the form of the Pickwick Club the officers were the same as the krewe, so Churchill was in effect the first president of the Pickwick as well.

Among the traditions of krewes as begun by Comus, the Captain would be the supreme power of the parading organizations. In his capacity as president of the group, Churchill may have been Comus' and therefore Carnival's first captain. The Comus Centennial book published in 1957 lists Churchill as such. As mentioned above, Miceli's book on the Pickwick Club stated that John Pope was the first captain. It may be that Pope had the title and Churchill had the power. Whichever, it seems clear that Churchill was Comus', and hence Carnival's, first real Boss. He would have likely been the most instrumental in molding all that was to follow. While the original six lit the torch, Churchill was the one who carried it.

Miceli's description of the early men of Comus/Pickwick seems to fit Churchill: "The members, most of whom were in their thirties, were well-to-do businessmen, active and full of life. The group was a close one. So intimately identified with each other were the members that it was like "one happy family."

Churchill, who was 30 at the time, was in the wholesale hardware business. His company, Taylor & Churchill, was located on Magazine Street. He and his wife, Martha, lived on St. Charles Avenue near Jackson Avenue. He was born in North Carolina. His father, Claudius Belden Churchill, was a physician. His mother apparently later lived in New Orleans, rented an apartment from her son and outlived him. He died relatively young in 1868; she died in 1872. Curiously, his mother's family name was Holliday and she was sometimes referred to as Lucy though she was also known, and listed in records, by the first name of "Louisiana." Thus the group that would mold Mardi Gras in New Orleans was founded by a man whose mother's name was Louisiana Holliday.

A.W. MERRIAM

He was not among the original six at Pope's Pharmacy nor was he there at the Gem, and he was not a marcher in the first Comus parade, but Albert Walter Merriam would become a towering figure in the organization.

Merriam, who was one of several young men who was invited to join after the first parade, was born in 1826 in Ware, Massachusetts. He would eventually become captain of Comus, serving from 1872–74. Merriam's first year as Captain was pivotal in the evolution of New Orleans' Carnival celebration, for in that year the Rex Organization was founded. As Captain of Comus, Merriam had a hand in starting Rex as did other Comus members. Rex would give Carnival a daytime parade, expand the participation in Carnival and give the season a public persona as opposed to the more secretive Comus. As Samuel Kinser would write in his book, *Carnival American Style: Mardi Gras at New Orleans and Mobile*, "Comus was incomplete without Rex. The private-society idea needed a civic dimension in order to survive in a democratically organized polity."

Among all the businesses of Carnival's founders, Merriam's was easily the most popular and the most visible. In 1865 Merriam bought the building on the Corner of St. Charles and Canal Street that before the Civil War had been the Merchants' Hotel and that during the War had been taken over to house Federal troops. Merriam converted the building so that the two upper stories were combined and made into an elegant billiards hall. Then, for a whopping $5000 he added a veranda that was 18 feet wide on Canal Street and 16 feet on St. Charles. The first floor was laid with mosaic tiles and housed various shops, including purveyors of wines, cigars, and an oyster house. Known as Crescent Hall, Merriam's billiards place would be an important gathering place for the overwhelmingly male downtown work force.

At the nearby St. Charles Hotel, located a block away from the billiards hall, the Rex Organization was founded, but one can imagine plans of upcoming parades and the details of Rex being discussed over billiards at the Crescent Hall. The building's place in male society would survive, eventually becoming the home of the Pickwick Club as it still is today. It would be on Merriam's galleries that the Comus courts of the future would watch the parades march by.

During Merriam's three years as Captain, Comus staged one of Carnival's all-time most controversial parades. The 1873 march was a political satire that poked fun at the Federal occupiers during those tense days of Reconstruction. Entitled "The Missing Links of Darwin's Origins of the Species" the parade depicted various occupiers as animals, including General Benjamin Butler, the head of the local Federal forces, who was shown as a hyena, and a cigar-smoking President Grant who was represented as a tobacco grub. The parade triggered a flurry of telegrams between New Orleans and Washington in an attempt to cool tempers. Charles Darwin himself was sent a copy of Comus' souvenir program and a local newspaper article attacking his theories. He was not amused, writing, among other caustic comments: "The abusive article in the newspaper amused me more than Comus."

On Mardi Gras night 1874, Merriam, as Captain, led the Comus parade. When he reached Crescent Hall at Canal and St. Charles he left the parade so that he could review the procession from the gallery. He saluted each float as it passed by. After the parade he went to the French Opera House for the Comus tableaux and then attended the post-ball supper. Then he entertained some friends at home until he retired around 3 a.m. Within a few hours he suffered a stroke, collapsed and never regained consciousness. On the afternoon after Mardi Gras, less than 24 hours after leading Comus, a funeral was held from his home at 587 St. Charles.

A resolution from the Pickwick Club published in a newspaper bemoaned the loss saying that he "leaves to us the heritage of his virtues and his goodness."

Albert Walter Merriam would be among the first of many generations of carnival organizers who lived for Mardi Gras.

VARIETIES THEATRE.

Varieties Theatre. The initial Varieties Theatre, where Comus staged its first ball in 1857, was at Gravier Street, between Carondelet and Baronne Streets. Illustrated here is the second Varieties Theatre which opened on Canal Street in 1871. The name was later changed to the Grand Opera House. (See Grand Opera House illustration, pg. 68.) Many tableau balls, including Comus, were held there until the building was razed in 1906.

2 INTRIGUE, CHIVALRY AND POLITICS AT THE TIME OF REX

ON THE EVENING OF DECEMBER 4, 1871 some of those who would be players in the formation of a kingdom gathered in a setting appropriate to the new monarchy—a theater.

Center stage was a man who had often played the role of a king but who, fate would have it, would win his spot in local history not for having played, but for having clothed, a ruler. It was Lawrence Barrett, the distinguished actor known for many roles, including that of Shakespeare's Richard III. One day soon he would lend a Richard III costume to be worn on Mardi Gras afternoon by the newly created King of Carnival, but on this evening his world was the stage. The occasion was the opening of the Varieties Theater, the second coming for that facility that had twice been destroyed by fire. This time, its new location, which would become known as the Grand Opera House, was a splendid building located on Canal Street. (Future generations would know the site as that of the Maison Blanche office building and then the Ritz-Carlton Hotel.)

Barrett, a performer of national stature, was given the title of manager of the theater. In that capacity, it was up to him to open what *The New Orleans Times* newspaper described the next day as, "the new and elegant temple of the drama." After the opening overture Barrett appeared in front of the curtain and delivered as an inaugural address a poem that began with these words:

The molten flood which down Vesuvius side
Poured desolation to resistless tide,
And left Pompeii where the Arts had birth–
A tomb of ashes on the breasts of Earth.

Those were words of despair written presumably to parallel the plight of the Varieties which had previously turned to ashes.

Sixty lines later the poem shined its light on the new theater:

A wooden scepter and a tinsel crown,
A pasteboard palace and a painted town.

Building toward an optimistic finale the poem ended with Barrett proclaiming:

Friends of the stage, this pleasing duty done,
Hope lights her torch with commendations won,
Our mimic scene on up-toe waits her ray.
Ring up the curtain!—This, kind friends—the play.

Barrett received the applause but the words were not his. They were written by an incredible character in New Orleans during the early 1870s—an adventurer, a poet and a journalist named E.C. Hancock. He was a man who spent much of his time behind the scenes although he was able to move people with his words. Through Hancock's efforts another curtain would soon rise in New Orleans and sitting behind it would be a lasting character known first as simply the King of Carnival but eventually more familiarly as "Rex," a jeweled monarch born in the spirit of "a wooden scepter and a tinsel crown, a pasteboard palace and a painted town."

For there to be a monarchy there must be a king maker. In 1872, at the time of the first Rex parade, Hancock was Associate Editor of *The New Orleans Times* newspaper. He is the pivotal figure in chronicling the evolution of Rex. Newspaper articles from the time, many probably written or influenced by Hancock, provide some indication of what was on the minds of the people who founded the Rex organization. Later articles would underscore Hancock's importance in creating the kingdom.

In 1921, as the Rex parade approached its fiftieth anniversary, a reporter for *The Times-Picayune* located Lewis Salomon, the man who served as the first King of Carnival. Salomon, who was 83 at the time, was living in Long Island, New York. The former Rex granted an interview that is of historic importance because he was one of the last living links to the men who in early 1872 gathered to start a new carnival parade:

"Well, in the lobby of the old St. Charles Hotel, a group of young men used to meet every night. Yes, our 'hangout' you might call it. There was Bob Rivers, Albert Baldwin, E.B. Wheelock, the druggist; W.E. Pike, the banker; Chris Mehle and his brother, William; C.H. Hyams, C.T. Howard, Durant Duponte," Salomon recalled.

Then, as though fate touched him on the shoulder, he added another name:

"Oh, yes, and E.C. Hancock, the big chief:

"Come to think about it again, Hancock was the life of the crowd and was really the originator of the Carnivals as we know them now.

"Hancock was Managing Editor of *The New Orleans Times*" Salomon said, perhaps mistaking the editor title since *The Times* of that day identified Hancock as Associate Editor. "Hancock was a brainy man," Salomon added, "and later it was through *The Times* that Carnival was kept alive."

Salomon continued with a vital piece of information about Rex's founding: "One night about two weeks before Mardi Gras of 1872 . . . the crowd was in the lobby of the St. Charles, and we got to talking about what we were going to do at Carnival.

"Someone—I'm sure it was Hancock—said: 'Now look here; why not make this Carnival a real affair?'

"At first we didn't think seriously about it, but Hancock insisted that all the promiscuous maskers and private clubs ought to be organized into a general parade.

"Of course money entered into the discussion . . ." Salomon continued. "When someone else in our crowd asked how he intended getting the money for the affair he promptly replied:

" 'Let Salomon do that!' "

For his efforts as fundraiser, Lewis Salomon would become the first Rex. But what is a king without a crown? Here too Hancock intervened:

"At the time we were getting ready for the Carnival, Lawrence Barrett, the tragedian was playing at The Varieties," Salomon remembered. "Hancock introduced me to Barrett while he was behind the stage as 'Rex, king of carnival.' We told Barrett what we wanted to do in the way of having a pageant and he agreed to help.

" 'I'll do all I can,' he told me, and he loaned me his Richard III costume and we located a crown, scepter and other paraphernalia in the wardrobe of the theater so that I could look like a regular king. The cloak, I recall, was a beautiful thing of velvet and ermine."

Only weeks earlier Hancock's words as bellowed by Barrett had opened the new theater. They would fit the moment when Rex received his crown as well:

"Ring up the curtains—this kind friends—the play!"

As is true with most of the men who founded Rex, Edward C. Hancock was not from New Orleans. The city, both before and after the Civil War, was not as much a town of native-born residents as it was a western outpost with an economic importance that drew people to it.

Hancock was a native of Philadelphia. When he died in 1893 an obituary described him as being "a member of the Hancock family famous in history." Presumably then Rex was founded by a kin of John Hancock who was also known for his written words, but more so for their size than for their fluidity.

When he was 22 Hancock moved to New Orleans. His first job was with a clothier. During the Civil War he served as a blockade runner working out of Nassau and Cuba. Another Rex founder, C. H. Hyams, did the same. Blockade runners tried to sneak past Union ships in the Atlantic to deliver medical supplies and gunpowder to Confederate forces.

Returning to New Orleans after the War he became a journalist, first with the *The Times*, then with a paper he established, *The New Orleans Herald* and finally with *The Picayune*. Claiming part ownership of that latter paper, he got into a protracted lawsuit. By 1876 Hancock was a special correspondent for *The New York Herald*.

In 1872, the year of Rex's founding, Hancock was 41 years old. He was young, but older than most of the other founders. Salomon was 33 at the time of his reign. Hyams was 34. Another founder, C.T. Howard, who in 1872 was manager of the state lottery and made a sizable contribution to the first Rex parade, was the same age as Hancock and was also a native of Philadelphia.

Curiously neither Hancock nor Salomon lived in New Orleans very long after the first Rex parade. By 1877 Hancock had moved to New York where he spent the rest of his life in various publishing ventures. In 1874 Salomon, a banker, had moved for his company, also to New York.

Hancock is now remembered because of his involvement with Carnival, but while he lived here he was better known as an outspoken journalist, so outspoken that in 1873 he was the target of an attack.

On the evening of Saturday, May 31, Hancock and three other men had met at the St. Charles Hotel around 11 o'clock. At midnight they had decided to walk to a nearby bar, "The Age," located at St. Charles and Gravier Streets. After leaving the saloon Hancock and the men returned to the St. Charles Hotel. There Hancock parted from the men and headed for the office of the *New Orleans Herald* where he then worked as an editor.

At the corner of Gravier and Camp Streets, Hancock was attacked by two men, each swinging what press accounts would describe as a "Baltimore Billy club or a similar instrument." With one blow he was struck on the "frontal bone" just above the eyes. The blow, newspaper accounts would say, cut through "his thick beaver" and left him with a cut an inch and a half long. Another blow struck him in the palm of his left hand. That blow caused him to fall over a box. He recovered, rose to his feet while the assailants delivered several more blows. Hancock began to run while shouting "murder!"

That might have been the outcome had passersby not heard the commotion. As pedestrians rushed to the scene the assailants fled. They were chased by several people but never apprehended.

It was an incident that made headlines throughout the city, including in the local French language newspaper *L'Abeille:*

LA TENTATIVE D'ASSASSINAT
CONTRE LE REDACTEUR DU "HERALD"

Also, in the local German newspaper, *Deutsche Zeitung:*

RORDANGRIFF AUF EINEN EDITOR

And the story was picked up by the *New York Times* although the weapon, and the severity of the incident, differed in its telling:

A NEWSPAPER MAN ASSAULTED
NEW ORLEANS—About 1 O'clock this morning an unknown party using a slungshot (sic) assaulted E.C. Hancock of the Herald on the corner of Gravier and Camp Streets. Hancock received a severe but not dangerous cut in the forehead. His assailant escaped.

Most New Orleanians, however, probably read about the incident in *The Herald,* the paper Hancock was associated with at the time of the incident. On the front page of its Monday, June 2, paper

The Herald heralded the incident beginning with a three-deck headline:

A BOLD ATTEMPT AT ASSASSINATION
One Of The Editors of the Herald
Brutally Assaulted by Hired Ruffians
Another Attempt To Throttle the Press

In its exhaustive coverage of the incident *The Herald*, which first used the word "assassination" in describing the attack, noted that Hancock as well as other staff members had received threats including one that warned, as the newspaper put it, "that if a certain class of editorials were continued in *The Herald*, the editor would suddenly find himself in very serious trouble." The newspaper suggested that behind the assaults were certain parties who "have suffered by and dread the continuance of the exposure of their misdeed by the *Herald.*"

In its coverage the newspaper noted that although many people had heard Hancock's cry that night, no police came. The newspaper's own investigation suggested that the assailants were in fact local police.

What happened to Hancock apparently had nothing to do with his involvement with the Rex organization, but it does tell a lot about the tension of the times in which the Rex organization was created. The King of Carnival was born during Reconstruction.

Political tensions were extremely high in the city during the period that coincided with the first half-decade of Rex's existence, and that may be one of the reasons the organization was created. In a state that would always be known for the controversial nature of its politics, the years, 1872 and 1873 may have been the most controversial of all. It happened that in 1872 there was a gubernatorial election. The voting was so fraudulent that the near bankrupt state wound up with two rival governors and legislatures. Hancock, his friends and the newspapers he worked for seemed to represent a moderating influence. With the Civil War now over they were pro-Union at heart, although one could easily be pro-Union and still be outraged by the corruption, factionalism, and political manipulation of the Reconstruction era. A crusading journalist at the time could have easily found targets, and could have easily become a target in return.

Among the several newspapers published during Reconstruction was *The New Orleans Republican*. It was supportive of the party whose name it bore, although the party was badly split. One of the investors in the newspaper was Gov. Henry Clay Warmoth, a carpetbagger who saw to it that the newspaper got lucrative contracts for publishing state records. There were three factions within the Republican party— Warmoth headed what was known as the Liberal Republicans. Tensions were so high in 1872 that Warmoth, whose ascension to the governor's office had been backed by the Army of Occupation, chose not to run for re-election. He supported instead a fusion ticket headed by John McEnery, a Democrat, but that contained three Liberal Republicans running for other offices. Challenging them was another Republican ticket head by William Pitt Kellogg.

Though McEnery's ticket won the popular vote, a Federal judge issued one of the most criticized rulings in the state's history, order- ing that Kellogg should be seated. As '72 ended Louisiana had two governors. By May 1873 there had been riots throughout the state, including a violent demonstration in the upstate town of Colfax. On May 22, 1873, President U.S. Grant issued a statement publicly back- ing the Kellogg government and urging the "disorderly and turbulent people to retire peaceably to their abodes." That was nine days before the attack on Hancock. While it is uncertain what prompted the assault, newspapers would have been critical of the circumstances by which the Kellogg regime ruled and the heavy-handedness of the Federal occupiers. The period was clearly one of political violence.

In the days before the first Rex parade *The Republican,* which called itself the "Official Journal of the State of Louisiana," published on its pages some of Rex's edicts that told of the parade's coming. The newspaper seemed to be close to the Rex organizers. On April 30,

1873, only a month before the attack on Hancock, *The Republican* was quite supportive of Hancock's new newspaper:

THE NEW ORLEANS HERALD

". . . Rumor has placed Alexander Walker and Mr. Hancock, formerly of the *Times* in command of the editorial corps . . . These are all gentlemen of ability and experience, and no doubt a readable paper will be a result of their labors. *The Herald*, it is claimed, will be free from ring control, independent and fearless, while just and charitable. Politically, it will enter the lists as a 'free lance.'"

Beyond the crusading journalist, Hancock was a romanticist during an era when romanticism ruled like a medieval monarch at court. It may be that Hancock, the journalist, saw himself as a knight out to slay dragons.

New Years Eve, 1871: That day's edition of *The New Orleans Times*, the paper for which Hancock was serving as associate editor before moving to the *Herald*, had some curious listings. This was the last day of the year before Rex's birth. The King of Carnival would make his entry 44 days later.

Included that New Year's Eve was a chronological summary of newsworthy events from the previous year. Most of the listings were the sort of events that might be expected in a year-in-review listing:

- FEB. 23—Passage of the City Water bill.
- JUNE 3—The rear of the city overflowed.
- AUGUST 4—Large Fire in Milneburg, Lake End, First death by yellow fever.
- DEC. 1—Grand mass meeting at the Mechanics Institute of citizens to adopt measure of reform.

One can only assume Hancock's hand in preparing the list. Also included among the listed events were two items that seem totally out of context but that may, in retrospect, be quite revealing:

- MAY 18—Arrival of Horace Greely.
- JULY 15—Centenary celebration of the birth of Sir Walter Scott celebrated throughout the English speaking world.

Horace Greely and Sir Walter Scott, two men of different eras, nationalities and influences—what possible fascination could they cause?

E.C. Hancock would have been intrigued by Horace Greely whose name is one of those that people seem to vaguely remember from their history lessons, but are not sure what he did. One reason for the confusion is that he did so much. Greely, a native of Amherst, New Hampshire was a journalist and a politician. He began his political career as a Whig but later founded the Liberal Republican Party which, at the national level, opposed the Grant Administration.

As a journalist he was best known for having founded *The New York Tribune*. He used his paper's forceful editorial page to urge education reform and he wrote passionately against slavery. Greely's *Tribune* did much to develop anti-slavery sentiment.

During Reconstruction he became disillusioned with the corruption of the Grant Administration and its handling of Reconstruction. For that reason he founded the Liberal Republicans, the same party that Warmoth headed in Louisiana. The year 1872 was a presidential election year as well as that of the gubernatorial campaign in Louisiana. Greely ran as the Liberal Republican's candidate for president. He was attacked by the opposition with such velocity that he uttered one of the campaign's best quotes: Greely said he didn't know if he was running for the presidency or the penitentiary. In defeat he received 40 percent of the popular vote.

His visit to New Orleans in May 1871 had received extensive press coverage. The *Times* treated him with deference in one article and satirized him in another, both in the same edition. His itinerary included lunch at the Boston Club. Hancock would have likely met with the man who was the most famous editor in the nation. Did Greely the abolitionist and education reformer have an effect on the New Orleans Carnival?

One January 30, 1872, two weeks before the premiere of Rex, an item appeared in Hancock's paper, *The New Orleans Times*. It told of the coming of a new parade organization and began accordingly:

"According to Mr. Greely and all other great public lights, the raw material should never be wasted, and so think a few respectable, and public spirited, young citizens in regard to the display of Mardi Gras."

From there the announcement went on to tell about the collecting of "raw material": "Heretofore the maskers who generally are out in goodly numbers upon that day, have wondered around in small bands loosely all over the city. These they prepare to collect together at Canal Street, at three o'clock in the afternoon, and arrange into a procession. Bands of music will be provided, and at that specific hour the Chief Marshall and his aide propose to be waiting at the Clay statue to take charge of all arrangements . . . "

Continuing, the article provides more details about the parade. It ends with a burst of enthusiasm: "No doubt the announcement will stimulate the young people to greater efforts, and New Orleans will, this year, revel in a procession almost equal to the night display of the Mystic Krew {sic} of Comus."

In early November 1872 Greely lost the popular vote for the presidency. The candidate never got to hear the final electoral vote total. He died on November 29. On Dececember 4 of that year the local German language newspaper reported Greely's death and announced that flags would be flown at half-mast.

Among the most frequent hangouts of those who organized the first Rex parade were the St. Charles Hotel and the posh Crescent Billiard Hall owned by one of the most active of the early Rex organizers, Col. William Merriam. On Dececember 5, 1872 those two places were mentioned in a news item in *The Daily Picayune*:

IN MEMORIAM—A large number of vessels now in port, the Custom-House, the Crescent Billiard Hall and the St. Charles Hotel displayed their flags at half-mast yesterday in respect for the memory of Horace Greely . . .

Rex's founders had a relationship with and a respect for a man who was both an outspoken abolitionist and a critic of Reconstruction's excesses. The founders represented a moderating element during a turbulent post-war period still under the influence of the rifle,. Hancock probably liked Sir Walter Scott too, although Mark Twain did not. Because of that we may understand more about the sentiment at the time Rex was formed. In 1883 Twain's book, *Life on the Mississippi* was published. In a chapter entitled "Enchantments and Enchanters" Twain wrote of the New Orleans Mardi Gras and of Rex:

"All these people are gentlemen of position and consequence; and it is a proud thing to belong to the organization; so the mystery in which they hide their personality is merely for romance's sake, and not on account of the police."

Twain seemed to approve of Carnival, but not of romance, particularly Southern romanticism which he linked to the tales of knighthood and chivalry of Sir Walter Scott:

"(In the South) the genuine and wholesome civilization of the nineteenth century is curiously confused and commingled with the Walter Scott Middle Age sham civilization . . .

"It was Sir Walter who made every gentleman in the South a Major or a Colonel, or a General or a Judge . . . "

Twain despised the original state capitol building in Baton Rouge standing on the edge of the river like a medieval castle. And he knew who to blame:

"Sir Walter Scott is probably responsible for the Capitol building; for it is not conceivable that this little sham castle would have ever been built if he had not run the people mad, a couple of generations ago, with his medieval romances. The South has not yet recovered from the debilitating influences of his books."

Kings have always been a part of the carnival, tracing back to the Saturnalia and its other pagan ancestors. But the European, medieval representation of royalty, including knights, dukes and chivalry was likely influenced by Scott who was widely read during the age of Romanticism, that lasted well into the 19th Century. It is striking that in its New Year's Eve, 1871 edition of the *Times* its editors thought the centennial of Scott's birth worthy to be included with the other, mostly local events.

On New Year's Eve, 1872, at the end of the year in which Rex was founded, a new group, the Knights of Momus made their debut. The Knights theme was based on Scott's "The Talismen." Had Twain returned to Mardi Gras in 1885, two years after *Life on the Mississippi* was published, he may have raised a bushy eyebrow as the Rex title float passed. The theme that year was Scott's "Ivanhoe."

History usually favors those who stay around long enough to claim their place. Because Hancock left for New York only a few years after the first Rex parade, his importance would be overlooked. Over time it would be left to others to develop and grow the organization. Hancock's relative anonymity may fit into the spirit of the organization, for behind the throne, as is true with many carnival organizations, there has always been a person quietly working and whose identity has been kept secret. That person is the Captain.

Traditionally the Rex Captain, or prior to the use of that term, "the Manager," has been given the ceremonial name of "Bathhurst." That name may have been taken from either the First, Second or Third Earls of Bathurst. The Third, Henry Bathurst, 1762–1834, was the most interesting. He was a friend of William Pitt. During his career he was Lord of the Admiralty, Lord of the Treasury and Commissioner of the Board of Control for India. He was also secretary for war and secretary for the colonies. In that latter capacity he was actively involved with the abolition of the slave trade. Something else that the Southern Romanticists, if not Mark Twain, would have liked: In 1817 the Third Earl of Bathurst was made a Knight of the Garter, England's highest knighthood honor.

While in New York City, E.C. Hancock first established a news-paper called *The Truth*. After that paper failed, he worked for *The New York World* where he seemed to have had a lengthy and successful career. Later he established a magazine called *Family Fiction*. That lasted until he health began to fail. He was a widower and had no children. Hancock died May 30, 1893.

His obituary notice appeared in the New Orleans *Times-Democrat* the next day. Probably no one noticed it, but that date was exactly the twentieth anniversary of his being attacked on the streets of New Orleans. Most of the obituary notice concerned Hancock's career as a journalist. The final paragraph, however, contained some revealing information:

Prior to mentioning that Hancock had belonged to "one or two" social clubs in New Orleans and had been "well known and prominent" the article stated: "Mr. Hancock, while in New Orleans was an enthusiastic promoter of the Mardi Gras festivities, was among those who originated Rex, and was the original Bathurst."

New Year's Eve, 1871: On page one of *The New Orleans Times* a column about "Amusement Notes" reported on performers who were coming to, or going from, New Orleans. Lawrence Barrett, the Varieties Theater director had on the previous week opened in New York in "Julius Caesar." His role was that of Cassio. Playing Brutus in that production was Edwin Booth the distinguished actor whose late brother, John Wilkes, epitomized the turmoil of the era. Lotta Crabtree, so popular during that era that she was known simply as "Lotta," was performing in Memphis. At the same time Burlesque performer Lydia Thompson was on stage in St. Louis.

Attending one of her performances there was the Grand Duke Alexis Romanoff of Russia who was making his tour of America. Lotta, Lydia and Alexis: As fate would have it all three would be in New Orleans at the time of the upcoming Mardi Gras, all three would be cast in one of the season's most endearing legends. On that same page of the *Times* was a poem entitled, "The New Year." Its author? Edward C. Hancock.

Drawing from royal allusions the poem began accordingly:

Like monarch to his bed of state.
the Sun marched down the sky,
In gorgeous vestures richly drest,
A crimson baldric 'thwart his breast

Beginning the second stanza, Hancock provided an image of a images:

But marched the Day-god not alone,
beyond the even's gate;
With him an unseen pageant strode
Adown eternity's dark road.

His sixth and final stanza ends with still more regal illustrations:

As herald became dart forth to clear
The pathway of a bright NEW YEAR
Up to the throne from which, so late,
the dying Old year fled.

From the hand that held the pen a new monarch would come with the new year. He would match wits with Comus, a god of mirth who, in New Orleans, reigned at night.

There was no theme to the first Rex parade which, out of necessity, relied on spontaneity. Although the Confederacy was no more, Rex's premiere procession was certainly a confederation, a group of independent entities linked to a central figure. That figure was the King of Carnival (he was seldom referred to as Rex that first year) personified by Lewis Salomon draped in his borrowed Richard III cape, astride a steed.

For several days before Mardi Gras, the King's publicists had been, through the newspapers, taunting the public about the new parade and had called for the citizenry to join in. Mardi Gras was not yet a holiday, yet many businesses released their employees at noon that day. By two that afternoon a group of maskers and onlookers began to form in the vicinity of the Clay statue on Canal Street. Gradually a parade formed. At 3:15 the signal was given and the initial parade of the King of Carnival began. Covering the event was *The Republican* which on the next day published the order of the parade units:

- Mounted Police
- Music
- Section of Artillery, C.W. Squires
- Lord Chief Marshall of the Empires
- Attendants
- King of the Carnivals
- Attendants
- Lord of the Yeomanry
- Three hundred Maskers on foot
- The Pack
- Fatted Ox
- Music
- Lord of the Carriage, followed by sixty carriages filled with maskers
- Music
- Lord of the Vans, followed by a hundred carts, milk wagons, two and four-wheeled vehicles
- Lord of the Horse, followed by a hundred and twenty mounted maskers
- The Dan Rice cavalry
- Indiscriminate and miscellaneous rabble

Although *The Republican* had been, in the days prior to Rex's debut, supportive of the venture by publishing the King's proclamations, the newspaper sniffed a bit in its critique of the first parade, complaining that "there was too much order about it. Confusion, disorder and discord, both of color and of sounds, is the great beauty of a carnival procession . . ."

There was one element of the parade that the newspaper praised highly however—the group called "The Pack." These men seem to have been part of the King of Carnival's organization. Each wore a costume consisting of a wooden frame, approximately 33 inches square. A white cotton cloth was stretched across the frame. Each of the frames was then designed to represent four of a kind in a pack of cards: four aces, four deuces, etc. "The pack is comprised of gentlemen all fully identified with New Orleans," the newspaper reported. "Their object in making the display was to make the Crescent City attractive, not only to strangers but to citizens, and they succeeded admirably. The King of Carnival must certainly be proud of this playful Pack. May they play their jolly game next year."

That the Pack was part of the King's official family seems evident because the group had pre-parade duties that included making visits to the mayor and to newspaper offices, though time prevented the latter. The group's biggest moment though may have been as the parade passed Gallier Hall. There the Aces and other cards presented Govenor Warmoth and the Grand Duke Alexis each a gift—a pack of cards.

Might the Grand Duke have found the Aces to be wild, or merely Jokers? Either way, the revelers who wore the costumes were, as the newspaper alluded to, men of prominence in the city. They fit the profile of the Rex organizers, all of whom had either business or social connections, or both.

Lewis Salomon wore the borrowed robe of a royal literary character who caused tragedy. though he played the role of a far more jovial king named Rex.

Carnival had a new leading man.

Comus parade passing Gallier Hall, February 13, 1872. *This was a big date in the evolution of the New Orleans Carnival. That afternoon Rex had staged his initial parade. The Russian Grand Duke Alexis (depicted standing at the top of the reviewing platform) witnessed both parades. That evening Comus staged his ball in the newly opened Varieties Theatre on Canal Street.*

3 MYTH BUSTING: THE REAL REASONS FOR REX

ONE OF CARNIVAL'S most endearing legends has been that the first Rex parade was created as an entertainment for the visiting Russian Grand Duke Alexis Romanoff. The true reasons are far more complex. Pieces of the answer are found in the comments of two early Rexes and by looking at what was happening in other cities.

George Soulé's roots were in New England, roots that spread to New York State where he was born in 1834 and then ultimately to New Orleans where in 1856, having just graduated from a business school in St. Louis, he opened the Soulé Commercial College and Literary Institute.

As was true with many Northerners living in New Orleans at the time of the Civil War, he joined the forces of the Confederacy. Soulé was a Captain in the Crescent Regiment and fought at Shiloh, as did first Rex Lewis Salomon. There Soulé was wounded and captured. He remained a prisoner of war until he was swapped as part of a prisoner exchange at Vicksburg. He then rejoined his regiment.

After the war Soulé (who claimed to be a descendant of pilgrims that landed on the Mayflower in 1620) returned to his New Orleans school and became active in various community groups. One of those was the Rex organization. In 1887 he wore the crown as Rex, King of Carnival. During his professional career he authored several books with such lofty titles as; *Soulé's Philosophic Practical Mathematics, Soulé's*

New Science and Practice of Academics, and *Soulé's Partnership Settlements and Contractions in Numbers.* The Practical Mathematics book was hailed as being the most extensive book on the subject published up to that time.

A lesser known publication of Soulé's may be the most revealing in contemporary times. The undated pamphlet believed to be published c. 1909, was called simply, *The Carnival in New Orleans.* His text is a bit of a ramble hitting a range of topics, but it is clearly Rex-centered. At one point he offered his explanation of the origins of Rex:

"Some forty-eight to forty-four years ago grim-visaged war raged with all the its horrors between the Northern and Southern States of the union. This war produced animosities, jealousies, prejudices and dislikes in the minds of many people in the North and in the South. Forty years of peace have not fully effaced these animosities and the hearts of all the good people of our country."

Here Soulé presents Rex as a unifier: "To aid in the destruction of these elements of discord, dislike and dissension, and to enthrone in place thereof pure friendship, fraternal feelings and noble sentiments of esteem for one another is the higher and nobler purpose for which the Rex organization stands, and which it is striving to accomplish."

Soulé then hints at yet another purpose—tourism. "The management of the organization took advantage of the Carnival festivities to add eclat to its attraction while it directed its energies to the nobler work of bringing the people of all sections of our country to New Orleans. . ."

Throughout Soulé's essay the word "patriotic" was mentioned several times. In his closing paragraph this descendant of a pilgrim/former Confederate Army POW quotes American presidents:
- Grant: "Let us have peace."
- McKinley: "Let concord, not discord prevail."
- Wisely, the last words are left to Lincoln: "With malice toward none and charity for all."

Could Soulé's perspective on Rex's founding be merely the personal interpretation of a man who was Rex 15 years after the founding? Perhaps. But then there is the comment of the first Rex, Lewis Salomon, made in the 1921 *Times-Picayune* interview: "Carnival was being talked about, when the war was over, as a sort of tonic for the wearied South."

What then is to be made of the Grand Duke Alexis? Neither Soulé nor Salomon mentioned Alexis in their recollections. Newspaper accounts during the time of the first Rex parade do not link the Duke to the King. "Local Intelligence," a column in *The Republican* published on February 11, 1872, two days before Mardi Gras, did report on Rex and Alexis as dual budget items: "Our city fathers have made a small expenditure of the double purpose of receiving the Duke Alexis and celebrating Mardi Gras."

A frank and revealing earlier paragraph, however, that sounds like something written in modern New Orleans, probably hits closer to the practical justification for the new parade:

"We have published the several edicts issued by Rex, so our readers are posted on his intention," *The Republican* states. "One of the foremost considerations in this display is to make our city attractive, not entirely for citizens, but principally for visitors. Items of these things have gone abroad, and public attention has been drawn to New Orleans. This will bring hither not less than 15,000 people, and they will, on a low average, expend fifty dollars each, thus bringing capital to our city."

Building to a crescendo, *The Republican* continues: "Every visitor, on returning home, will give his less fortunate neighbors a pleasant or glowing account of the wonders of the Crescent City. Next year the number of visitors will be doubled; and so our city will be benefitted. For this reason residents should make the celebration as attractive as possible, and Rex has pursued the right course."

As the Grand Duke legend would have it, the Rex parade was intended to be a one time event to honor the visitor. In fact, *The*

Republican was already counting the next year's tourism dollars.

It may be that the truth is more honorable than the legend. Rather than a group of men spending their time to stage a parade for a twenty-two year old Duke, whose keenest interest in America seemed to be to hunt buffalo, they were trying to market war ravaged New Orleans. Rex's centennial book, *If Ever I Cease to Love: One Hundred Years of Rex 1872–1971,* by Charles Dufour and Leonard Huber, suggests uncertainty about the Duke story. The book's very first paragraph asks: "If His Imperial Highness, the Grand Duke Alexis Alexandrovitch Romanoff had not included New Orleans on his American tour of 1871–1872 one may well ask, would Rex have come into being?"

In a later paragraph the authors give deference to the Grand Duke legend but concede, "The records are somewhat obscure as to the precise origin of the first Rex parade."

Another classic carnival book, *The Mistick Krewe: Chronicles of Comus and His Kin,* author Perry Young supports the Alexis story but sees broader purpose as well: "This movement, **justified for other reasons,** (emphasis added) was a hasty and tardy effort to do honor to the Grand Duke."

Among the other reasons cited by Young:

- "There had been three murders on Mardi Gras 1871 directly attributed to the mode of celebration."
- "The fame of Comus had spread and was drawing crowds of visitors from afar, to the great embarrassment of the Krewe whose entertainments were 'designed for the amusement of themselves and their immediate friends.' Another society was needed."

Rex's organizers were not oblivious to the Grand Duke. While none of the edicts issued by the founders, and published in local newspapers in the days preceding Mardi Gras, mentions Alexis, Rex did issue a whimsical proclamation to welcome the Duke.

Should Alexis be placed on a pedestal in Rex history? Yes, clearly, although it may be a different pedestal than previously used. Instead of being the cause, Alexis may have been one of the catalysts, another reason to hasten a parade that was probably going to happen anyway. The Duke did view the parade and by his presence he added true royalty to the event. His appearance on Mardi Gras, 1872 romanticized Rex, and perhaps legitimized Rex's claim to be the King of Carnival— one sovereign acknowledging another.

That tourism was at least one of the factors in the founding of the Rex organization might be evident in the backgrounds of the founders. Among those that Lewis Salomon, the first Rex, listed in the 1921 interview as being part of the gatherings at the St. Charles Hotel from which the Rex parade evolved was Robert Rivers. Listed on the tax roles for that period is the name Rivers, Foley & Co as being part of the ownership of the hotel. Another founder, Chapman Hyams was, at the time of his death in 1923, mentioned by *The Times Picayune* as having his "heaviest holdings" in the St. Charles Hotel Company, for which he was identified as being the principal owner. The St. Charles Hotel in which Rex was founded was actually the second at that site on the 200 block of St. Charles Ave. The first was destroyed by fire in 1851. The second met the same fate in 1893. The *Picayune* obituary gave Hyams strong credit for building the third hotel which would last until the 1970s when it was razed. (Eventually the Place St. Charles office building would be constructed on that site.) Hyams, a member of the New Orleans and New York Cotton Exchanges, as well as member of the Boston Club, was also reported to be "the largest stock owner" in the Louisiana Jockey Club. During his New Orleans visit, Grand Duke Alexis stayed at the St. Charles Hotel and was the honored guest at a Jockey Club luncheon .

Whatever the circumstances were that gave birth to a King of Carnival in New Orleans in 1872, they were also in place during the same year in Mobile, Alabama where there was no Grand Duke Alexis.

Mobile's role in New Orleans' Carnival history is typically both exaggerated and misunderstood. While it is true that Mobile's Cowbellians inspired the founding of the Mistick Krewe of Comus in New Orleans, the old carnival in Mobile did not survive the Civil War very well. What eventually emerged in Mobile was a New Orleans style carnival celebration borrowing even from Rex's colors of purple, green and gold. In 1872 the Mobile Carnival Association was formed creating its own version of an omnipotent carnival monarch, King Felix.

In Soulé's essay he refers to a New Orleans Carnival Association having been founded in 1872 under the direction of Rex. Why is it that carnival associations were formed in two cities in the same year with each establishing an overall king figure? If Mobile did not need the presence of a Grand Duke to inspire the birth of Felix, did New Orleans need the Duke for there to be a Rex? Post-war re-structuring of celebrations as a way of drawing visitors to cities may have been part of a national movement. As we will see in Chapter Four, during the same decade the tradition of Mummers parades in Philadelphia, which trace back to the 1700s, also fell under the guidance of an association, and for similar reasons—to bring discipline to the celebrations and to attract visitors.

There were close ties between New Orleans and Mobile in the 19th century. Both were Southern cotton ports with a French heritage. Both experienced a formalized carnival celebration initiated by Americans more so than French Creoles. In both cities the Creole had the traditions, but the Americans had the money and initiative. They created the parades.

There was also a social force at play.

As of 1871 there were two organized parading carnival organization in New Orleans, The Mistick Krewe of Comus and the Twelfth Night Revelers. The groups were like bookends to the seasonal calendar. The latter marching on the evening of Mardi Gras, the last day of the Carnival season, the former parading on the evening of Twelfth Night, the season's first day. In 1866 a city clerk in Mobile named Joe Cain spearheaded a disorganized spoof of a parade designed to poke fun at the Federal Occupiers. Joe Cain's procession became known as the People's Parade. Joe Cain Day is still celebrated in Mobile on the Sunday before Mardi Gras.

By 1872 there seemed to be growing pressure for a people's parade in New Orleans too, not one as informal or rebellious as Joe Cain's but one that would expand participation in Carnival. The history of Carnival in the Gulf South is like a rock thrown into a pool. The impact causes a series of circles each spreading a little further.

Comus' role is significant because some Rex founders also belonged to the Mistick Krewe. The infant Rex was nourished by Comus' expertise. But it was in the nature of Comus and the mystic organizations in Mobile to be private, not only internally, but externally as well. Carnival needed a persona, a public figure, a benevolent monarch. Though many Rex members walked in the same high society circles as those in the mystic clubs, Rex would play a more civic role. Consider again the words written by Perry Young in *The Mistick Krewe:*

"The fame of Comus had spread . . . Another society was needed."

Many kings have come to power with less civic calling than did Rex. On the practical side Rex gave the New Orleans Carnival a day parade. That in turn had financial benefits for the city as circulars promoting New Orleans and its expanded Carnival were distributed by the railroads along their route. On a civic side Rex allowed another circle of participation in Carnival. On the political side Rex gave Carnival a public figure in counterpoint to the cherished secrecy of the mystic clubs. On a ceremonial side Rex greeted a Grand Duke. Kingdoms are created by circumstance but few can count among their circumstances one that Rex could. His was a kingdom that came into existence partially because a troubled republic needed it.

*1898 Rex parade on **St. Charles Avenue.** The King of Carnival's theme that year was "Harvest Queens." Pictured is float number nine entitled "Cotton." Note the mule-drawn floats and the spoked wagon wheel.*

MYTH BUSTING:

BEFORE MOBILE—THE CITY AND CULTURE THAT REALLY INFLUENCED CARNIVAL

THOUGH OVERLOOKED IN HISTORIES of the American Carnival, Philadelphia, that ultimate of American towns, was the most important city in the development of the early American Carnival. Surprisingly, the European roots to the American Carnival also stretch to Sweden.

In antebellum America Philadelphia had a major influence on the South. It was one of the richest and closest Northern cities to the region. From there people, ideas and traditions flowed easily.

Known of course as the city of the Declaration of Independence, there was a frivolous side to Philadelphia as well. Going back to that city's earliest period, each New Year's day miscellaneous bells and other noisemakers were heard along the streets as a group called the Mummers paraded. A 1981 article in *Smithsonian Magazine* explained it accordingly:

"Historically, the New Year's day Parade results from a blend of cultures that thrived in the city from the early half of the 17th century through the early part of this one. English roots go back to 15th century Christmas Mumming Plays. (Mumming comes from the German word *Mumme*, meaning disguise or mask.) Local tradition has it that as early as the 1620s the Swedes and Finns in Tinicum—now a southwestern section of the city—celebrated the New Year by shooting off guns (they were often called "the shooters"), banging pots and pans, and making a clamor as they visited neighbors after Christmas."

Another article published by a Mummer's string band traced the European origins and made reference to a mythological character that was also part of the New Orleans Carnival:

"It started in the late 1700's. When the Swedes came to Tinicum, just outside of Philadelphia, they brought their custom of visiting friends on 'Second Day Christmas,' December 26. Later they extended their period of celebration to include New Year's Day, and welcomed the new year with masquerades and parades of noisy revelers. The traditions of other nationalities were also present. The use of masks and different costumes were carried over from the Greek celebrations of King Momus, the Italian-feast of Saturnalia, and the British Mummery Play."

Just as America would be a melting pot of people, the city that was the country's cradle would become a melting pot of celebrations. In Philadelphia the post-Christmas festivities took the form of the Mummers wearing costumes, making noise and parading on New Year's Day.

Now the scene switches to Mobile, Alabama, the town that first influenced New Orleans' Mardi Gras parading tradition. It was there that on New Year's Eve night, 1830, a group of men, including a one-eyed reveler named Michael Krafft, were about to step into history.

Perry Young, in his classic book, *The Mistick Krewe: Chronicles of Comus and Kin* told of a dinner at a downtown Mobile restaurant organized by Krafft. The celebrating continued well past midnight: "At the approach of dawn they continued their frolic on the streets and at the important hardware store of Griggs, Barney & Company encountered irresistible temptation in the shape of rakes, gongs, cowbells, and horns which early-morning clerks had displayed in front of the store.

"The young gentlemen armed themselves with these rakes, cowbells, horns, and perhaps, some other instruments, and proceeded to parade on the streets with clang and clamor."

It may be that the events were less spontaneous than they

appeared to be. Young might not have known, or appreciated the significance of the fact that Krafft was from Philadelphia. Michael Krafft would have been very familiar with a tradition of parading and hell-raising on New Year's Day. In his own way, he brought mummery to Mobile where it would be metamorphosed into a group called the Cowbellians. Gradually their march would be institutionalized and shifted to coincide with the French celebration of Mardi Gras. The history of celebrations is that of one culture building on the other. That's what was happening as the American Carnival evolved.

Next we go to New Orleans where the celebration of Mardi Gras had been mostly lavish balls and sorry street spectacles. As Young reported, some Mobile Cowbellians came to this city and didn't like what they saw. Borrowing on their Cowbellian know-how, they were part of the group that, in 1857, established the Mistick Krewe of Comus. That was the beginning of the New Orleans Carnival parading tradition as we would know it—a tradition that would become part of the universal image of Mardi Gras.

A style of parade evolved in New Orleans that was different from anywhere else, but the link through Mobile began in Philadelphia where a variety of European celebrations were synthesized into the Mummers. Their marches were the first steps of Carnival. From that setting, Michael Krafft went to Mobile. As Young so poetically put it: "The seeds sown by Michael Krafft have persisted. His mystic progeny are legion. Many have appeared on the scene and disappeared after periods of varying success. But they are copies, not of a Carnival which once held sway in Italy or France, but of a pageantry initiated by Krafft and his gay fellows, and deftly fitted into the ancient Carnival of New Orleans by an evolution of its own."

In New Orleans, the Philadelphia influence would be felt in other ways. The event that crystallized Mardi Gras in New Orleans as a major celebration happened 15 years after the first Comus parade with the founding of the Rex organization in 1872. Two of the founders; E.C.Hancock and C.T. Howard, were from Philadelphia. As we have seen, Rex was founded primarily as a cure for Reconstruction

NOW FOR SOMETHING MODERN!

Lundi Gras is **NOT** *an old tradition. It started in 1987*

EXPLANATIONS OF LUNDI GRAS too frequently say that the tradition traced back to 1874 when Rex began arriving by river. Those arrivals stopped in 1917. So Lundi Gras is usually described as a revival of an old tradition. In fact, though it has quickly become widely-used, the phrase "Lundi Gras" was not commonly part of the local Carnival language until 1987. In that year Rex did revive his river arrival, but that was only part of the new Lundi Gras festivities that included fireworks, concerts on the river and, for several years, Proteus marching down Poydras toward the river. Prior to '87, the night before Mardi Gras was just known the night before Mardi Gras. From 1874–1917, Rex's arrival was never referred to as Lundi Gras. The accurate statement would be to say that Lundi Gras started in 1987 as a series of events that included the Rex arrival. Accurate statements, however, sometimes have a hard time getting recognized.

and to coordinate into one the miscellaneous groups that had been parading on Mardi Gras. In Philadelphia the sentiment was shockingly similar as noted in the string band's article: "In the 1870's the nation was recuperating from a Civil War and what had been an uncoordinated group of neighborhood celebrations turned into an area wide parade with two main groups of participants." Might Hancock and Howard been inspired to found Rex by the news from back home?

Philadelphia's Carnival influence likely spread toward the Atlantic. In the Bahamas a celebration called the Junkanoo is experienced each New Year's day. For the occasion, locals dress in costumes and join marching clubs to parade and celebrate. Junkanoo written histories suggest African links and there may be, but the Mummer influence is overwhelming. In colonial days the Bahamas were governed by the territory of the Carolinas. Ships from Philadelphia would have made many stops on the islands. Junkanoo is probably Mummery with an African spin. Curiously, Junkman and Comus may have had common ancestors.

While French Canadians, bless them, brought the phrase "Mardi Gras" to the new world, and French settlers informally celebrated the day, the parades were largely a Protestant creation. Among the last names of the original founders of Comus: Todd, Addison, Pope, Shaw, Ellison, Churchill, Lay, Smith, Handing, Wood, Coiners, Ellis, Ross, Ferguson, Newton, Campbell, Murphy and Butler. There is not one recognizable French name among them.

Among the Rex founders, the key person, E.C. Hancock, a descendent of John Hancock, was not likely Catholic. Lewis Salomon, the first Rex, was a convert to Catholicism from Judaism. The others had mostly Anglo-Saxon names. As we have seen, one early Rex, George Soule, was a descendent of the pilgrims who landed on the Mayflower. Soule was from New York, Hancock and fellow founder C.T. Howard were from Philadelphia.

All of the Northerners fought in the Civil War for the Confederacy but their Yankee roots probably made them eager for the city to rejoin the Union's mainstream.

Curiously this phenomenon of Protestants embellishing a Catholic holiday is not unique to New Orleans nor this country. I once spoke to a Dutch sociologist who had studied European Carnivals. He noted that there were several Catholic villages where the Protestants had been the main force behind the Carnivals. Why? One possible explanation is that the Protestant work ethic introduced an entrepreneurial spirit into Carnival by creating an event to boost local economies. Remember too that Anglo-Saxon cultures also had a tradition of post-Christmas winter celebrations. As the world expanded, their festivity would be absorbed under the French term "Mardi Gras." And finally, though the French Catholics have the image of having a good time—Protestants want to have fun too.

Rex ball 1879. *This is an illustrated detail of the event which was held at Washington Artillery Hall, previously known as Exposition Hall. The building was on St. Charles Street between Julia and Girod Streets. A state office building currently occupies the site. Rex that year was William Mehle. His parade theme was a comic representation of "The History of the World."* THE HISTORIC NEW ORLEANS COLLECTION

1974.25.19.377

5 MYTH BUSTING: THE TRUTH ABOUT THE COLORS

DURING THE CIVIL WAR BATTLE of Manassas, General P.G.T. Beauregard of New Orleans became concerned that the Confederate units did not have appropriate battle flags so that one unit could be identified from the other. Beauregard sent word for a flag to be designed. Several designs were submitted, including one from E.C. Hancock. Aiding Beauregard in the selection was a former staff member, Colonel William Porcher Miles. The Colonel rejected one of the favored designs because it was contrary to the laws of heraldry. Miles suggested a flag instead that was similar to Hancock's proposal —red, with blue bars and white stars. From the incident we learn two things about future Rex founder E. C. Hancock. He had an interest in designing flags and he was aware of the laws of heraldry.

A lingering mystery in the Rex organization has been the true meaning of Rex's, and hence Carnival's, official colors—purple, green and gold. Through the years there have been many explanations, but never one that could be verified. The most common, and easiest answer, contemporary explanation has been that the colors stand for justice, faith and power, but one might wonder why those qualities were so special to the Rex founders. Why not faith, hope and charity? Or trustworthy, loyal and helpful?

Not only is there uncertainty about the significance of those three words, neither is there certainty about their association with those colors. There have been many other associations of words to colors that varied considerably. Under Grosse Rules of Military Antiquities, purple represented fortitude; green, good hope and yellow, honor. Are fortitude, hope and honor any less virtuous than justice, faith and power? A book on *Signs and Symbols of Christian Art* has purple, green and gold representing triumph, power and pure light respectively. The meanings are clearly in the imagination of the beholder.

A 1950 newspaper column by Pie Dufour in the *New Orleans States* seems to have popularized the "justice, power, and faith" explanation although Dufour wisely did not totally embrace it. In an earlier column Dufour had explained that there was no acceptable explanation for the origin of the colors. A few days later he heard from a local librarian who drew his attention to Rex's parade in 1892 which had the theme "Symbolism of Colors." Each float displayed a color and a meaning. Floats seven, twelve and eight depicted purple, green and gold respectively with justice, faith and power, in that order, assigned as the meaning of each. A flowery statement issued by Rex, and published in *The Times-Picayune* that year, proclaimed those three words to be the meaning of the official colors.

Dufour wondered how the 1892 Rex members knew what was on the minds of the founders 20 years earlier. He suggested that the true origin might be simply that the colors looked good and that they had, as a *Picayune* editorial on the eve of the first parade noted, a "delightful contrast." Arthur Burton LaCour's 1952 book, *New Orleans Masquerade: Chronicles of Carnival* expressed similar uncertainty about the origin of the colors but dismissed some other theories that were based on the Grand Duke's visit:

"Contrary to prevailing reports the colors of Rex were not based upon the old Russian flag which consisted of three horizontal stripes—white, blue and red. The Imperial standard was yellow, emblazoned with a double-headed eagle, surmounted by the Imperial Crown."

In the Rex Centennial book, *If Ever I Cease to Love: One Hundred Years of Rex, 1872-1971* authors Pie Dufour and Leonard Huber further dashed the prevailing theory although it would nevertheless survive. After telling about justice, faith, and power being linked to the 1892 parade they argued: "This of course is an *ex post facto* explanation, and one may be certain that the colors were selected in 1872 because they were gay and colorful and not because of any symbolism as explained by Rex two decades later."

One reason that the origin of the colors has been so difficult to discover is that the original Rex organizers never offered any explanation. They called for the colors purple, gold and green to be displayed, but never said why. That supports Dufour's and Huber's contention that the colors had no meaning, Surely if they did the poetic philosophers among Rex's founders would have said so. But why those particular three colors? For that there has been no answer—until one-fourth of the way into Rex's second century.

While doing research for the Rex 125th anniversary book *Marched the Day God: A History of the Rex Organization* (The School of Design 1999), lightning struck and we were able to deduce an answer. The missing link had been found.

Finding the answer began with another question: Why three colors? Why not one? Two? Five? Or ten? Was there anything significant to the number three? The key to that answer may have been hidden in the edicts issued by the Rex founders in the days preceding the first Rex parade, and published in *The Republican.*

Those edicts contained good natured verbiage that suggested a true sovereign. "His Royal Highness" issued orders preparing for his arrival. In the minds of the founders a king must have a kingdom and a kingdom must have a national flag. All of the national flags that the Rex organizers would have been most familiar with: United States, Great Britain, France, were tri-colors. It was probably inconceivable to them that a flag should be anything else but a tri-color.

That resolved then, which three colors? Here we might assume that a certain three colors were immediately dismissed: red, white and blue. Not only were those colors already taken by the above mentioned nations (as well as the Confederacy), they were, ever since the

Netherlands carried flags of red, white and blue in its war against Spain, the colors of revolution and a republican form of government. Those colors were hardly appropriate for an absolute monarch such as what Rex presented himself to be.

Given that there would be three colors, and given that the founders probably ruled out red, white and blue, what then should the colors be?

One color seemed obvious, purple, for that color has traditionally been linked to royalty. From here the selection process takes on a life of its own. The key word here, and a word that has been missing from attempts to solve the colors' origin is—"heraldry." Dating as far back as the fifteenth century, the rules of heraldry governed the symbolism of coats of arms and hence flags and banners. The men of Rex, educated and steeped in the romanticism of monarchy, would have been familiar and respectful of heraldry, which also governs color selections.

According to heraldry, the "fields" in a heraldic device should consist of "metals" and "colors." The metals are either silver, represented by white, or gold. And indeed every national tri-color has either white or gold. So then for one of Rex's choices the selection was narrowed to two. Should the metal be gold? Or should it be white? The choice of gold seemed obvious, especially with white already in such common use.

Now with the metal settled, how about the colors? According to heraldry, there are only five acceptable choices. In the context of Rex they are startling, The acceptable colors are red, blue, purple, green and black. With purple being a logical choice and with gold as the metal, the final choice came down to two combinations: purple, gold and green or purple, gold and black. The choice seemed obvious.

But now there's a concern. According to heraldry a metal should never touch a metal and a color should never touch a color. It would be improper, for example, for a flag to be, red, blue and white. Yet, Rex's flag is often spoken of as being purple, green and gold, a heraldic *faux pas* placing a color on top of a color. Does this disprove the heraldry theory? No, it supports it because in the days preceding the first Rex parade when the Royal edicts were published, the field, as first mentioned in Edict XII, was stated as being, in this order, "green, gold, and purple." Over time the order of the colors would be changed in popular verbal usage, yet when Rex first pronounced them they were in perfect heraldic order. (The combination of colors does have the extra benefit, as Dufour/Huber suggest, of looking good together.)

Could there be another answer to the meaning of the colors? Perhaps, but any other answer would have to contend with the colors fitting so perfectly into heraldry.

What then should the simple answer be when the colors' origin is asked? The problem is that the answer is not simple, certainly not as simple as "justice, faith and power." But it only strengthens Rex's monarchical status to the truth, and that is, like all great sovereigns, the colors are based on the laws of heraldry.

Case closed.

First Rex parade photograph. *This image is believed to be that of the first Rex parade in 1872 as it turned from Canal Street heading down St. Charles Street. (If so it is the only known photograph of that parade.) Though archives identify the photo as having been taken in 1866 there was no day parade of that magnitude prior to Rex. Riders are wearing Bedouin costumes known to be worn in the parade. Note the size of the crowd and that the tradition of spectators wearing costumes had not been established yet.*

LOUISIANA STATE MUSEUM

6 MYTH BUSTING: ALEXIS, LYDIA AND THE ANTHEM

CARNIVAL'S MOST ROMANTIC LEGEND is that of the Grand Duke Alexis and burlesque singer Lydia Thompson. (Burlesque in those days did not mean strippers but more of a satirical, only slightly naughty, leggy entertainment.)

As the story goes, *If Ever I Cease to Love* became the New Orleans Carnival's anthem when it was learned that Alexis was smitten for Lydia. Alexis had heard Lydia sing that song when they both happened to be in St. Louis. There he had seen her perform "Blue Beard," a show that contained several numbers including that one. Through an envoy, Alexis had even sent Lydia a bracelet. The legend continues that the bands in the first Rex parade, having heard of Alexis' fondness for Lydia and the song, played *If Ever I Cease to Love* as they marched past the Duke. The legend added a plot device to the saga of Rex's evolution—a love story, more so a love story matching royalty with a showgirl. Now for the truth:

Alexis may have become infatuated while in New Orleans, although with a different woman. Lotta Crabtree, who at age 25 had already had won fame performing in the Gold Rush camps near San Francisco, made a return engagement to New Orleans. On this trip she was performing a show called "The Little Duchess" at the St. Charles Theatre. Alexis attended Crabtree's performance. He was so charmed that he sent an aide to express his congratulations to the actress. The Duke had also accepted a well-publicized invitation to see Lydia Thompson's show, although he missed the performance, opting to stay at the Jockey Club where luncheon activities ran into the evening.

Overlooked in the Lydia-Alexis romance theory is the simple fact that there was a significant age difference between the two. Alexis was 22, Lydia was 36. If Lydia had a friend among those who were part of Rex's first days, it may not have been a duke but a king. Thompson's 1872 visit to New Orleans was her third tour here, so she was well known in the community. Lewis Salomon, Rex I, was active in theater. He would have had many opportunities to make her acquaintance.

A curious statement published in *The Times* on Feb. 6, 1872, a week before Mardi Gras, revealed the first Rex as being a ruler with love on his mind. A series of tongue and cheek articles, likely written by E.C. Hancock, had been printed each telling about the mysterious "King of Carnival" preparing for his debut. The article that day even dealt with the King's social life:

"His majesty has never married, giving as an excuse that this state should not be entered into until experience has sobered the liveliness of youth and all the wild oats have been sewn. We give this latter piece of information for the benefit of the ladies who are already overwhelming His Majesty . . .

"It is well to note in the latter connection that the national air or anthem of the Carnival Dynasty, for many centuries past, has been, as is at present, "If ever I cease to love."

Besides its playfulness, the statement is significant because it alone disproves the legend about that *If Ever I Cease to Love* spontaneously evolved as Rex's anthem when on Mardi Gras bands began to play it for the Duke. As early as a week before, the song was already proclaimed as the anthem.

Truth is, the song preceded Lydia to New Orleans. According to Arthur Hardy's 1989 *Mardi Gras Guide*, the original version of the song, which was published in London in 1867, was written by a certain George Leybourne whose other big hit was *The Man on the Flying Trapeze*. Depending on where it was performed the lyrics were changed, quite often to be local and topical (i.e., May the Grand Duke Alexis ride a buffalo through Texas), but always expressing an undying love. In 1871 Thompson adapted the song for her burlesque, "Blue Beard." In that same year the song was published in at least two song books; the *If Ever I Cease to Love Songster* and the *Half-Dime Series of Choice Music*. With that the song spread throughout the country. New Orleans, a port city with a vibrant theater community, would have been among the first places to receive new music.

That the song was clearly popular in New Orleans months before either Lydia or Alexis arrived was made evident in a poem that was published in *The Times*, Nov. 6, 1871 more than two months before Rex's premiere:

A SONG FOR SENTIMENTALISTS
(Not a bit more silly than some we have heard lately.)

If never I cease to love,
The moon may change her hue,
And 'mid the stars above
The sun no more burn blue,
Among the woodland trees,
The whales their song may cease,
And oysters at their case,
May keep their beds in peace.

If never I cease to love,
The cows may catch the croup,
While of the turtle dove,
Lord mayors no more make soup,
The frogs may plow the main,

The tigers soar far above,
The rain may cease to reign,
If never I cease to love.

Chances are Hancock wrote the poem. Obviously a spoof, its existence suggests a familiarity with the published version of the song. To Hancock the music's playful lyrics and silliness might have been perfect for Carnival. *If Ever I Cease to Love*, contrary to legend, was not played for the Duke during the Rex parade. For him, the bands played the Russian National Anthem. The song was played instead for the King of Carnival at his reviewing stand. Auguste Davis, a New Orleans music teacher, developed a march arrangement for the song, all the better to enable the bands in the original Rex parade to follow the decree that the tune should be played while "passing in review before His Majesty."

That evening, at the Academy of Music, the theater where, on other nights, the popular Lydia Thompson was appearing, a Grand Bal Desguise was staged by a group called La Coterie Carnival. The Grand Duke began his evening by watching the parade of the Mistick Krewe of Comus wind along the city's old streets as though drawing a curtain on the Carnival season. Alexis attended the Comus Ball at the Varieties Theatre, then, once the krewe dance was complete, moved on to the Academy of Music where he was greeted with the Russian National Anthem. From there he attended another ball, this one at the St. Charles Theatre where he was reported to have stayed until two o'clock of Ash Wednesday morning. So moved by the day's events that had begun with Rex, the *Times* boasted in its Wednesday edition of "a new era in the long history of Mardi Gras festivities." The newspaper added that "the advent has not only been brilliant, but successful" so much so that "the thousands of delighted people who were not slow to express their enthusiasm can fully testify."

Rex did not stage a Carnival ball in its first year. Many of the organization's founders probably attended the Comus Ball that evening. Rex himself, his reign over and now a civilian in the person of

Lewis Salomon, most likely spent the evening at the Academy of Music where a ball was being staged by a group called La Coterie Carnaval. He was listed as a "Manager" of that organization as well as a member of its invitation committee. Salomon and the Grand Duke quite likely met at the ball that night although we will never know if Alexis knew he was meeting Rex. (The identity of the first Rex had been kept secret throughout that Mardi Gras.)

Possibly in that number at La Coterie's ball was Lydia Thompson who, because of the ball, would have had the night off from her gig at the Academy. If Alexis did greet Lydia at the ball however, it was probably the only time he saw her in New Orleans for, legends to the contrary, the Grand Duke royally snubbed her.

On November 18, 1908 a procession moved along the Champs Elysees in Paris. With full military escort the body of the Grand Duke Alexis was taken from his home in Paris to a Russian church where a funeral service lasted nearly two hours and then to the Gare Nord railroad station from which a special train would take Alexis to St. Petersburg. By bizarre coincidence, six days later, in London, a funeral service was held for Mrs. Alex Henderson who the world had better known as the actress Lydia Thompson. Lost in the obituaries was the role the two had played 36 years earlier when both happened to be in New Orleans at the time that a kingdom was born. After New Orleans their paths went in different directions, but during their lives Lydia and Alexis were the subject of love stories both real and imagined.

Kings being immortal, Rex still marches to the anthem declared by edict for his 1872 debut. As the anthem is played the legends of Alexis and Lydia survive for, history aside, in the Kingdom of Carnival, they never ceased to love.

Interior Stairway to the Grand Opera House (detail). *Located on Canal Street between Dauphine and Burgundy Streets, the new building which opened in 1871, was also known as the Varieties until its name was changed to the Grand Opera House in 1880. Comus helped christen the new building by staging his ball there in 1872, the year of the first Rex parade. The building was eventually demolished to make way for the Maison Blanche department store which is now the site of the Ritz-Carlton hotel.*

7
MYTH BUSTING:
A KING AND
A PRAYER

LEWIS SALOMON'S SELECTION to be the first Rex would launch a curious footnote in New Orleans Carnival history, a tidbit that, like much of Carnival history, is not exactly correct. It has been written, and repeated, in an ironic sort of way, that the first Rex was Jewish—an unusual selection given prejudices of the time and given Mardi Gras' Christian origin. In fact not only was the first Rex a Roman Catholic by conversion, but, according to family descendants, he was a very devout Catholic.

What is true about Salomon's roots is that on his father's side he is descended from a very prominent American Jewish family. His great grandfather, Hyam Salomon, was a Polish immigrant to the American colonies who would became a major figure in his new home's Revolutionary War. Twice sentenced by the British to be executed because of his undercover work on behalf of the colonies, Hyam Salomon escaped. A successful merchant, Salomon became a major financier of the Revolutionary War by raising money and by sacrificing much of his personal fortune to the cause. George Washington, Benjamin Franklin and the other Founding Fathers were among his acquaintances and admirers. Financing the War broke him, but after the War he opened a brokerage firm and recouped some of his losses. He then sacrificed much of his newly made wealth by helping support the start-up government and by underwriting charities.

FROM THE HORSE'S MOUTH

WHEN FIRST-REX DESIGNATE LEWIS SALOMON and Rex founder E.C. Hancock went to the Varieties Theater to borrow Shakespearean actor Lawrence Barrett's Richard III costume, the king to-be was impressed: "The cloak was a beautiful thing of velvet and ermine," Salomon would recall. Costumes for the various dukes were taken from the company's wardrobe. The first parade created some situations that future Rexes would be spared. There was no Rex Carnival Ball. After the parade the various members went their own way including Salomon who was listed as a "Manager" involved with La Coterie, one of the several other balls that night. And, there were no floats. Salomon rode a horse that was apparently a bit ornery. In 1921 he would recall the ride in his interview with *The Times-Picayune:* "Turning onto St. Charles at Canal, my horse stood on his hind legs and almost threw me. A moment later he shook his head and threw froth from his mouth all over me, and, alas, the beautiful velvet and ermine robe. I fear it was ruined."

Barrett's reactions are not known though we would assume he might recommend that future Rexes should ride a float.

Though born and raised Jewish, Lewis Salomon's life changed dramatically during one week in 1862. On a Wednesday he became a soldier; on Friday he became a Roman Catholic. Salomon, who was twenty-three at the time, worked at his father's private banking business located at the corner of Carondelet and Gravier Streets, but the 1860s were a time when young men throughout the politically divided nation were being called to arms. On Wednesday, March 5, Salomon enlisted as a private in Company E, Crescent Regiment, of the Confederate Army's Louisiana Infantry. Two days later, Friday, March 7, he walked up the steps of the Immaculate Conception Church on Baronne Street (known commonly as Jesuit Church) to be baptized as a Catholic.

Among those assembled for the ceremony were two all-stars of local Catholicism. One was J.J. Duffo, the Jesuit priest, who administered the sacrament and who, in 1853, had distinguished himself by caring for Yellow Fever victims. The entire New Orleans-based Jesuit

REX'S WAR BRIDE QUEEN
AND HER MOTHER-IN-LAW

REX DID NOT HAVE A QUEEN until his second year. In 1873 the reigning Rex (E. B. Wheelock) selected a woman from the audience, Mrs. Walker Fearn (Fanny Hewett). The debutante tradition had not begun yet so the first queen was the only married woman to have sat on the throne. Walker Fearn, a lawyer who had served as a diplomat to Brussels during the James Buchanan administration, was well known in New Orleans. He had met his future wife and queen to-be while serving in the Confederate military in Texas. His mother was such a prominent socialite in Mobile that the book, "Cotton City: Urban Development in Antebellum Mobile" used her as an example of important hostesses during the 1830s: "Mary Walker Fearn, wife of Dr. Richard Lee Fearn, gave receptions for such local guests as Governor John A. Winston, the surgeon Claude Mastic and the writer Theodore O' Hara. Distinguished Americans and European visitors also found welcome in the Fearn home."

community of that year had been stricken by the fever, except for Duffo, despite his having slept and eaten in a hospital hall on call to minister to the stricken, including his fallen brethren. The other was Thomas Layton. Church tradition calls for the person being baptized to have a sponsor, usually a layman. Layton was one of Solomon's sponsors. He was such a church insider that he served as Treasurer of the Archdiocese's Peter's Pence, a program to raise funds to support the church.

Salomon's Catholic leanings may have come from his mother, Adeline Sapporo, who was Catholic. His baptism into the church, two days after joining the Confederate Army, might be seen as the spiritual equivalent of hedging his bets, or it might have been a family tradition. Salomon's younger brother, Alexander, had been baptized at Immaculate Conception, also by Fr. Duffo, in 1861 when he was 12.

According to Salomon, his selection to be Rex was made by E.C. Hancock, a newspaperman with a flair for the literary, who was

A RELATIVE'S COLLECTION

PETER LANDAY, A GREAT-GRANDSON OF SALOMON. collected items once used by his relative. (Landay, a resident of Los Angeles, visited New Orleans in 1999 and attended the Rex Ball, though unannounced.) His collection included a wallet of Salomon's that contained invitations to various Confederate-related anniversary functions held in New York City. Like World War II veterans visiting the National World War II Museum, Civil War events were a catharsis for its old soldiers, including Salomon who fought at the Battle of Shiloh and who lived his life with memories of battles and of a reign.

the main force behind the creation of the parade. Salomon served as financier for the fledgling group, having the responsibility for raising funds. One of his techniques was to make a series of "hold-up" calls to "public spirited men and friends" asking each to put up $100 toward the cause. "Then I would promise to make them dukes," he would later recall, "and more than 50 put up the money that way." Hancock's selection of Salomon to be the first Rex was likely in appreciation of the latter's money-raising ability.

Hancock might have also been amused that the fund-raiser for the first Rex parade was a great grandson of the fund-raiser for the American Revolution.

(Curiously, Hancock was a descendant of John Hancock. Along with Salomon, two of Rex's founders were descendants of key figures in the American Revolution. Yet, both young men fought for the Confederacy against the nation that their ancestors had founded. Their leanings, however, were in keeping with their relatives' spirit. They too might have seen themselves as creating a new nation by breaking away from the control of another government. In those days the concept of the United States as a country that could not be dissolved had not yet taken hold. The South represented an opportunity for people to redefine themselves. That feeling could have applied to religion as well as to politics.)

In 1874, two years after his Rex reign, Salomon moved to New York City where he would marry and where he would stay. Because he was only thirty-three at the time of his reign and because he would live a long life, Salomon's recollections would prove essential to chronicling New Orleans Carnival history.

E.C. Hancock too would relocate to New York City where he continued to work in journalism. Though he was clearly the creative force behind Rex, his legacy would be forgotten. Salomon, however, returned to witness Mardi Gras six times during his long life and was always welcomed by the Rex organization.

Salomon would become a member of the New York Stock Exchange. His adult life would be lived as a Catholic, including sending a son to Xavier High, a Jesuit school in New York.

Jesuits were an influence in Salomon's life. A Jesuit baptized him, and he was a supporter of the Jesuit-based Church of St. Aloysius in New York. According to descendants of Salomon, there was apparently a rift between their great grandfather and the St. Aloysius church in later years, though the cause is unknown.

In the end his paternal roots embraced Salomon. Lewis Salomon died May 4, 1925 at age eighty-seven. He was buried at Shearith-Israel in New York—a Jewish cemetery. Why he was buried in a Jewish rather than Catholic cemetery is uncertain. Speculation among researchers and family members suggests that since he was survived by his wife, Theresa Frank, who was Jewish, it would have been natural for her to want to have him buried where she too would one day be interred.

Lewis Salomon was a divided man who was a product of a divided nation. He had the benefit of achieving immortality because, one day in 1872, his kingdom had come.

French Opera House. *Comus (1869) and Twelfth Night Revelers (1870) were the first Carnival organizations to use the building which was originally called The New Opera Hall until its name was changed in 1880. During its sixty years of existence many krewes held their carnival balls there. The building, located on Bourbon Street at Toulouse (now the site of a hotel), was destroyed by a fire in 1919.*

THE HISTORIC NEW ORLEANS COLLECTION

1979,325,5859

8 THE SON OF NIGHT AND THE SHEPHERD OF THE SEA

FROM THE BEGINNING Momus seemed destined toward Chaos.

By the end of the 19th century there were four established parading organizations in New Orleans; Comus (1857), Rex (Mardi Gras, 1872), the Knights of Momus (New Year's Eve, 1872) and Proteus (1881). (Twelfth Night Revelers, which had started parading in 1870, marched for the last time in 1876.) Each of the three that followed Comus was very much influenced by it, drawing membership and leadership from the Mistick Krewe as well as expanding participation for others. While Rex served a broader civic purpose as demanded by his title "King of Carnival," Momus and Proteus frolicked more in the tradition of Comus. Each would stage night parades cloaked in secrecy and enriched by traditions. Each during their first half-century would also be embroiled in a controversy, one similar to a situation Comus had faced, the other in a head to head stand-off with Comus.

Momus was a popular mythological choice among educated young American males of that day. In 1871 a group called the Knights of Momus premiered as part of the Galveston, Texas Mardi Gras. The Momus name had also frequently been linked to Philadelphia's Mummers celebration as well. (And still is. In the year 2000, the Mummers theme was "Circus Momus.")

Since Momus was the Greek god of laughter, ridicule, farce and sarcasm as well as the Son of Night, he was a natural for being a favored god of the partying set. His having been expelled from Mount Olympus added an admired touch of abandon to his image.

Like Comus, Momus was linked to an exclusive men's luncheon organization, the Louisiana Club. In post-Civil War New Orleans, Carnival was regenerating itself.

Momus strayed from the beginning. His decision to parade on New Year's Eve, while consistent with early parades in Mobile and Philadelphia, was outside the boundaries of the Carnival season which stretched from Twelfth Night (January 6) through Mardi Gras. (Some even saw the decision as a way of getting a jump on the Twelfth Night Revelers.) For whatever Momus' strategy might have been, it did not last. After its 1873 parade, Momus gave up his New Year's Eve spot; one reason being that the women attending its tableau too often had to leave early to prepare for New Year's day, another was to get a date closer to Mardi Gras. In 1876, Momus reappeared, this time on the Thursday before Mardi Gras—a date to which it would thereafter be linked.

Arthur Burton LaCour in his classic book *New Orleans Masquerade*, described the founding Momus members as "youthful gallants and mature scions of cultured forbears, emulating the esoteric and exclusive societies that produced the triumphant pageants and tableau balls of the Mistick Krewe of Comus and Twelfth Night Revelers . . ." Carnival during the 1870s was played out with Reconstruction in the background. In 1877, during the administration of Rutherford B. Hayes, Reconstruction ended, but Momus had the last laugh. Featuring floats, some of which were so wide that walls in the den had to be broken to release them, thus delaying the starting time to 10 p.m., Momus marched to the theme of "Hades: A Dream of Momus." This, one of Carnival's all-time famous parades, satirized national political leaders. Just as Comus had delivered punches at Reconstruction bosses four years earlier with its "Missing Links to Darwin's Origin of the Species" parade, Momus caused a furor. Some political authorities vowed vengeance. As LaCour pointed out however: "Secrecy was inviolable and the names of the Knights who participated in the masquerade were not obtainable, so the whole country joined in the laughter of the god of ridicule."

But the outrage had its impact. After the parade, Carnival krewes abandoned political satire in their themes. A century passed. Then, on the Thursday before Mardi Gras 1977, satire reappeared in a parade. As though clemency had been issued from Mt. Olympus, Momus was back with the barb. The God of ridicule was liberated.

Proteus was founded in 1881. Like Momus, the krewe's formation bore the thumb print of Comus. The Mistick Krewe had created such a sensation with its colorful yet mysterious nighttime march that more young men wanted to be involved. With the blessing of the Comus captain, six members of the Mistick Krewe joined forces with other aspiring revelers to form the krewe named after mythology's "Old Man of the Sea." (Proteus was also known as the "Shepherd of the Sea" because of his chores as herdsman of Poseidon's seals.) Drawing many of its early members from the Cotton Exchange, Proteus was the only one of the three night parades not associated with a luncheon club though one could assume that many of the Proteus riders dined in the same exclusive halls of Comus and Momus members.

From the beginning, Proteus coveted the Mardi Gras eve slot. (The term "Lundi Gras" was not commonly used until 1987 with the return of the Rex landing and the inauguration of related events at Riverwalk.) Proteus' original constitution even spelled out that the purpose of the organization was to stage a masked parade and ball, "on the Monday night before Mardi Gras each year."

Plans to debut the parade for the 1882 Carnival moved swiftly until it was discovered that a paid employee had taken off with the funds. Determined to parade nevertheless, the members of the new group agreed to assess themselves to make up for the lost funds. That resolved, on February 20, 1882 the Krewe of Proteus premiered. "The brilliant illuminations on the streets through which the procession passed last night added not a little to the brilliance of the scene," *The Times-Democrat* proclaimed.

Though fathered by Comus, a famous incident in Proteus history involved a stand-off between the two krewes: Much of what is known about early Proteus history is through the efforts of historians, especially Charles L. "Pie" Dufour who wrote the krewe's centennial book: *Krewe of Proteus: The First Hundred Years.* Among the stories told is that of the incident in 1890 when Comus returned to the streets after having not paraded for five years due to financial reasons. During that time, Proteus had moved to Comus' slot on Mardi Gras night. But when Comus returned, Proteus refused to give up the position. The organizations traded sarcastic notes with each other before both marched on the evening of Mardi Gras. As fate would have it, the lead elements of the two parades intersected each other at the corner of Canal and Bourbon Streets. "Nothing resembling coolness prevailed," Dufour wrote, "when the Irish captain of Comus and the Creole captain of Proteus confronted each other, each excitedly shouting defiance. Although the two were friends of long standing, they threatened each other with their riding crops as the Proteus captain gave the order to cut through the parade." The incident ended when a masker in the crowd, who had connections with both krewes and was known by both captains, defused the situation by grabbing the bridle of the Proteus captain's horse and moving it away.

What happened that night is one of Carnival's most told stories, but the peaceful resolution likely had historical impact that transcended story telling. Because Comus had dropped out for five years due to money problems, the Mistick Krewe was in danger of losing not just its parade spot but its place in history as though the link had been broken. Proteus and Comus would continue to spat with and tease each other over the next year but likely more in the spirit of fraternity brothers who, though at war in intramural competition, are ultimately bonded by being socially connected. Proteus would return to his proper spot and Comus to his. The friction of the time would be forgotten, as would the embarrassing gap in Comus' history, and the Mistick Krewe would rightfully be remembered as the father of it all.

In 1892 Proteus returned to its Monday night position, a slot it would hold for exactly 100 years before announcing, in the face of political tension, that it would cease parading. The decision, for the good of Carnival, proved to be of short duration.

Something new was added to Carnival in 1893 when Twelfth Night Revelers (which continued to present a ball after ceasing parading) extended the stage over the lower floor at the Grand Opera House. Seats at the rear were for women who were to be called for a dance by krewe members. In that same year Proteus embellished the idea by providing sectioned reserved seating near the dance floor for those who would be called out. Thus Proteus gets credit for introducing the concept of "call-outs" to New Orleans society balls. Other krewes, including those senior to Proteus would adopt the practice. Proteus, the newest of the old-lines, was making its mark.

After its 1877 "Dream of Hades" parade, Momus marched through the rest of the 19th century with little controversy. Its themes to follow were clinically mild, such as in 1878 and '79 when the Knights marched to "The Realms of Fancy" and "A Dream of Fair Women" respectively. We'll never know for sure if the Knights were drawing a tongue in cheek parallel to carpetbaggery with their 1883 theme of "The Moors in Spain" which told about the outsiders' invasion of the Iberian Peninsula. Momus' Queen that year was Winnie Davis, daughter of former Confederate President Jefferson Davis. Since Momus started having Queens in 1881, none had a bigger, or more politically charged, name than Davis. (While it is not unusual for one girl to serve as Queen of two or more organizations—especially once the debutante system began—never since has anyone sat on old-line thrones nine years apart. In 1892 Winnie Davis reigned as Comus' queen.)

During the forty-three years of the 19th century beginning with Comus' initial march in 1857, Carnival's parading krewes had quadrupled. Comus, Rex, Momus and Proteus would forever be referred to as the "old-line" krewes. Of the four, none would weather the transition from the 1800s to the 1900s as dramatically as Proteus which suffered frost-bitten agony one year and an almost comedic prestigious visit the next year.

On the day before Mardi Gras, 1899, morning temperatures were reported as having varied between 6.7 and 11 degrees. Proteus had been preparing for its traditional Monday march, but that would not happen that year. It was so cold that the mules would not pull floats, the livery stable operators would not release their horses on the streets.

Proteus took the unusual step of canceling both its parade and ball and rescheduling both to the Friday after Mardi Gras. But it wasn't the same. The solemnity of the first Friday of Lent had already set in. Like a Christmas carol sung out of season, the change just didn't seem right. The public mood was about as cold as the weather had been a few days earlier. Proteus' last Carnival of the 1800s had ended with the charm and color of an ice cube.

For the first Carnival of the 1900s, however the weather was much kinder. Anticipation was high. The *Picayune* proclaimed that many distinguished visitors were expected for the revelry including the Governor of West Virginia and his personal and official families.

One role that Carnival would play through the years is that of protocol ambassador by welcoming dignitaries representing other countries. Rex greeted the Grand Duke Alexis in 1872 and the Duke and Duchess of Windsor would be honored guests at the Rex ball in 1950. In 1900 the city prepared to welcome a visiting diplomat who was from mysterious China and thus conjured images of the exotic and the unusual. His name was Wu Ting Fang and he held the lofty title of China's Envoy Extraordinary and Minister Plenipotentiary to the United States.

According to Dufour, at 10:00 a.m. on the Monday before Mardi Gras a delegation gathered at the L & N train station to greet the arriving ambassador. The *Picayune* had gushed that the Chinese minister and his diplomatic staff will be, "naturally, a center of interest, and preparations are actively in progress for their reception and entertainment. They will form a brilliant and picturesque group, and will lend a strangely cosmopolitan flavor to the occasion."

As hoped for, the visit did prove to be a success although the local newspapers differed over whether the envoy's name was Wu Ting Fang or Ting Fang Wu; and despite the fact that rather than arriving with the expected diplomatic staff that would form a "brilliant and picturesque" group, the minister was accompanied only by his male secretary. Then there was the gaffe created by the secretary being a man of slender build with what the *Picayune* described as a "smooth delicate face." Because he was also wearing a flowing Oriental robe, the secretary appeared to some western eyes to be a woman. A pair of those eyes belonged to police Captain Dick Walsh, who was in charge of the crowd security detail. The captain, assuming the ambassador's traveling companion to be his wife, politely lifted his cap and said, "Good day madam, why haven't you brought your little boy?"

Fortunately ambassadors are trained to be skilled at diplomacy. Having overheard the question, the minister winked at the secretary who took that as a sign to make a joke out of the situation. "We decided to leave the boy behind," the secretary responded. A reporter for the *Picayune's* rival, *The Times-Democrat* wrote that "When Captain Walsh was enlightened later on, there was some hearty laughter."

That seemed to set the mood for the rest of the trip. Later, the Oxford educated ambassador (who spoke fluent English, though, curiously, with a German accent) was honored at a reception at City (Gallier) Hall, then was taken to the river end of Canal Street to witness Rex's arrival by boat. From there it was back to Gallier Hall to watch the Proteus Parade. That night he was escorted to the French Opera House for the Proteus Ball.

This was an era when the press placed higher priority on the artistry of parades than on the amount of trinkets thrown. Writing of the Proteus march and its theme "Tales of Childhood," The *Picayune*

MOMUS, GOD OF LAUGHTER

Ella Wheeler Wilcox

American Author and Poet

1850–1919

Though with gods the world is
cumbered,
Gods unnamed, and gods unnum-
bered,
Never god was known to be
Who had not his devotee.
So I dedicate to mine,
Here in verse, my temple-shrine.

'Tis not Ares,—mighty Mars,
Who can give success in wars.
'Tis not Morpheus, who doth keep
Guard above us while we sleep,
'Tis not Venus, she whose duty
'Tis to give us love and beauty;
Hail to these, and others, after
Momus, gleesome god of laughter.

Quirinus would guard my health,
Plutus would insure me wealth;
Mercury looks after trade,

Hera smiles on youth and maid.
All are kind, I own their worth,
After Momus, god of mirth.

Though Apollo, out of spite,
Hides away his face of light,
Though Minerva looks askance,
Deigning me no smiling glance,
Kings and queens may envy me
While I claim the god of glee.

Wisdom wearies, Love has wings—
Wealth makes burdens, Pleasure
stings,
Glory proves a thorny crown—
So all gifts the gods throw down
Bring their pains and troubles after;
All save Momus, god of laughter.
He alone gives constant joy.

Hail to Momus, happy boy.

declared that the pageant was, "a production which has never been sur-
passed in the characteristics of artistic beauty and splendor." The
Times-Democrat pronounced that the twenty magnificent floats "were
highly spectacular." The newspaper added that nothing "happier in
expression or more gorgeously beautiful in execution was ever seen on
the streets of New Orleans during Carnival season than the parade of
Proteus."

Proteus experienced a happy beginning to a century that would
NOT have a happy ending. In the ten decades ahead, Carnival would
expand, crowds would become dazzled by new krewes with bigger

floats from which riders dispensed bigger beads. Values and attitudes would change. And then, in the last decade of the 20th century the unthinkable would happen: Proteus, and two of its brothers, Comus and Momus, all born in the 1800s and molded by the familial and social traditions of a genteel era, would disappear from the parade route. For the moment though, the gods were playful.

Mardi Gras, 1898. *Apparent minstrel parody in the vicinity of the Rex parade, approx-imately the 1900 block of St. Charles Avenue.*

ZULU ENTERS
THE STAGE

PYTHIAS WAS IN BIG TROUBLE. He had been condemned to death for plotting to kill Dionysius I, Potentate of the ancient Sicilian city of Syracuse. Before he was to be executed, however, Pythias begged to be given leave so that he could take care of his personal business. Damon, Pythias' good friend, offered his own life as ransom in case Pythias did not return. Dionysius agreed. Pythias could have spent the rest of his life free at the cost of sacrificing Damon, instead, though facing many obstacles on the way back, he returned to accept his punishment. He arrived just as his friend was about to be put to death. Here the tale might have ended tragically except that Dionysus was so impressed by the loyalty of the two men who had been willing to sacrifice their lives for each other, that he set both free. Thus were two lives spared and, as told through the centuries, thus was another legend born. The names of Damon and Pythias would endure as symbols of true male friendship.

In 1859 Justus Henry Rathbone, a teacher in Eagle Harbor, Michigan, saw *Damon and Pythias,* a play based on the 4th century B.C. Greek myth. Rathbone was so moved by the story of male friendship that he thought it might provide an inspirational name for a fraternal order.

Secretive men's societies were very popular in the United States during the 19th century. Alexis de Tocqueville had noticed the phenomenon as early as 1832 when he wrote that in a nation lacking established hierarchies, the "independent and feeble citizens" sought strength through association. A century after Tocqueville, Historian Arthur M. Schlesinger, Sr. described America as a "nation of joiners," Schlesinger scoffed at the fraternal groups: "The plain citizen sometimes wearied at his plainness and, wanting rites as well as rights, hankered for the ceremonial, grandiloquent titles, and exotic costumes of a mystic brotherhood."

Rathbone himself was a member of the Masons and the Order of Red Men. His idea to start a new fraternal order was delayed by the Civil War's onset, so it was not until 1864 in Washington, D.C., where Rathbone worked as a nurse during the war, that the first lodge of the newly named Knights of Pythias was formed.

Founded in the capital city of the Union during the heat of the Civil War, the new Order had a stated mission of healing wounds and lessening the hatreds from the strife. President Abraham Lincoln was advised of the group's mission and praised it "for teaching people to love one another, and portraying the sanctity of the family and loved ones."

Nevertheless the membership of the Knights of Pythias, as was common at the time, was limited to white males only.

Quickly the Pythians spread to other cities. There was something about the brotherhood that was appealing across color lines. Male blacks wanted an organization too. Richmond, Virginia, once the Capitol of the Confederacy, was the setting in 1869 when a new group with a bulky but all-inclusive name was formed: "The Knights of Pythias of North America, South America, Europe, Asia, Africa and Australia." A law suit by the original Pythians sought to block the use of the name by claiming that it was used without authorization. The suit failed. Despite the global references in the new order's name, its membership was largely black and it would come to be more commonly known as "the Colored Knights of Pythias."

Like its reluctant brother organization, the Colored Pythians grew quickly, particularly throughout the South where the Federal fist still prevailed in the form of Reconstruction. Besides its mission of benevolence and fraternity, the fledgling brotherhood also offered one other service in high demand among blacks—burial security. In an age when blacks did not have easy access to insurance and to burial polices, and when the funeral process was very much segregated, many societies offered burial benefits. The Pythians had an extensive burial bureau, funded by members' dues, that handled funeral expenses. A companion bureau paid an endowment to a Knight's widows.

New Orleans became the national hub for black Pythianism. At one point the office of the Supreme Chancellor, a certain S.W. Green, was located there.

In 1908 the Pythian presence in New Orleans became quite prominent with the construction of the Pythian Temple at the corner of Gravier and Saratoga Streets. (Today Loyola Avenue, the building, which still stands has most recently been known as the 2-3-4 Loyola building. A facade distorts the building's original character.) Said to be constructed by a group of black businessmen at a cost of $201,000. the nine story building had an office, barbershop and bank facilities on the first floor. On the second floor was a theater.

Several years later a roof garden would be added to the building. That space would become a popular location for musicians playing that hot new sound evolving on the streets below. In Chicago the music would be given the name of "Jazz" but the Pythian's roof garden and the surrounding neighborhood were the music's incubators. Sidney Bechet, A.J. Piron, Papa Celestin and eventually Louis Armstrong would perform on the roof of the Pythian Temple. Their sounds echoed through the neighborhood made famous by South Rampart Street but that was also part of the rowdy, lively area today referred to as Black Storyville. The neighborhood was the center for nightlife and entertainment among the city's blacks whose options were otherwise limited.

That's why the second floor Pythian Theater was important. The facility was a safe place for New Orleanians of color to seek entertainment without the indignity of being relegated to the balcony.

As was also happening among white males, black men were seeking security and bonding from being a part of small groups as well as the bigger brotherhoods. One group was known as the Tramps. Its headquarters was near the Pythian building in the rear of a restaurant/bar in the 1100 block of Perdido Street. One evening in 1909 some of the Tramps went to the Pythian Theater to see a musical comedy performed by a group called "The Smart Set." Included in the comedy was a skit entitled "There Never Was and Never Will Be a King Like Me." The skit was about a tribe known as the Zulus.

Of all African tribes the Zulus of South Africa were the best known. They had achieved fame in 1879 when, at the Battle of Isandhlwana, a Zulu army of 20,000 overwhelmed a British force. Suffering nearly 1300 deaths the British that day experienced their worst colonial defeat ever. Ultimately the British would win the war and the Zulu kingdom would be divided, but the 1879 victory had given the Zulus an image of pride and resistance.

(Curiously the origin of the word "Zulu" is much more passive. In the native language it means "Heaven." The name was originally given to one of the founding chief's sons and eventually to the tribe whose pastoral area became known as "Zululand.")

For the second time in the evolution of Zulu's history a name would be inspired by a play. Just as the word "Pythias" had been influenced by a stage production in 1859, exactly fifty years later a comedy viewed at Pythian Hall would inspire the Tramps to retreat to their meeting hall at 1100 Perdido Street and emerge as "Zulus."

There is no record of how many of Zulu's founders were Pythians, but one could reasonably expect that there was a Pythian influence, at least as a model for a men's club. (A later Zulu, Louis Armstrong, revealed in his autobiography that he was a Pythian.) In that neighborhood the Pythian Temple building cast an imposing presence.

On Mardi Gras 1909, the group formerly known as the Tramps, which had started parading in 1901, premiered as Zulu. Its first King was William Story. According to the Zulu's organization's own history, "the group wore raggedy pants, and had a Jubileee-singing quartet

TRIBAL WARFARE IN DIFFERENT CONTINENTS

W HEN THE ZULUS OF SOUTH AFRICA massacred the British on January 22, 1879, the shocking outcome made worldwide news and established a reputation for the tribe. The battle, however, was not the era's only example of a tribal group slaughtering the army of a more powerful invader only to eventually be subdued.

In South Dakota, only two and a half years earlier, June 25, 1876, a combination of the Sioux and Cheyenne tribes had massacred General George Custer's army at the Battle of the Little Big Horn. In South Africa and in South Dakota, both battles were bumps in the Victorian era as the forces of mighty nations spread across continents.

Curiously, both battles would have links to the New Orleans Mardi Gras. The Zulu name would become part of the local Carnival; George Custer had attended the first Rex parade in 1872 in his capacity as escort to the Grand Duke Alexis.

Also, in New Orleans the tradition of Mardi Gras Indians would evolve among blacks. Southern blacks felt a kinship to American Indians whom they regarded as being fellow victims of discrimination. Though blacks in New Orleans would have been familiar mostly with the less flashy Choctaws, the colorful, feathery costuming that inspired them was that of the American Plains Indians as seen in the traveling Buffalo Bill Wild West shows. At those shows cowboys and Indians would recreate battles to the roar of the crowd. As is often true in Carnival, history had become theater.

in front of and behind King Story." The king wore a lard can as a crown and waved a banana stalk as a scepter.

From the earliest days, the Geddes and Moss Funeral Home on Washington Avenue, which serviced the black community, was a part of Zulu. The building became the site where Zulu Kings and Queens would toast each other.

Zulu's mission was more than just to parade. The group would also assume the all-important social aid function. Its formal name would say it all by combining a bit of black pride, a bit of compassion and a bit of fun: "The Zulu Social Aid and Pleasure Society."

On September 30, 1916 the organization was officially incorporated. It is from that date that Zulu has counted its anniversaries. The date is almost sixty years since the first discussions to establish the Mistick Krewe of Comus. By 1916 Mardi Gras had yet another monarch in the Carnival empire. He would wear a crown like all the others, but he looked ever so different.

EPILOGUE

THOSE WHO GATHERED at Pope's Pharmacy in 1857 concoct-
ed a powerful potion. Within six decades after the formation of the
Mistick Krewe, the elements that would define the New Orleans
Carnival had come in place—Comus set the template, Rex created a
daytime event and established a people's king, Momus and Proteus
provided for expansion and Zulu who made Carnival more democrat-
ic and certainly more politically justifiable.

All would have their triumphs and setbacks along their march
into the future. Comus suffered financial problems early in its existence, stopped parading, re-formed, reclaimed its Mardi Gras evening
parade spot but eventually ceased parading after a controversial discrimination ordinance in 1992. Through it all, the Mistick Krewe
maintained its paternal status in Carnival history and its mystique.
Like a European monarch, Rex would take seriously both his lineage
and his civic duty—acknowledging high society and providing leadership for Carnival during its crises. By the 1950s the Rex parade had
declined in quality, but in the '60s the organization began a comeback
by expanding its membership base, enhancing its parade and even
repopularizing—its, and hence Carnival's, anthem, *If Ever I Cease to
Love.*

Momus, would be the most impish of the founding brothers
though cautiously so. He waited a century after his controversial
"Hades—A Dream of Momus" parade before, in 1977, returning

with the satirical barb as though to assure that the humorless Reconstructionists were no longer around. Of all the founding krewes Momus was the most directly linked to a luncheon organization, the Louisiana Club. Though still staging a ball, the Knights' parade never returned after the 1992 civil rights ordinance. Carnival observers, however, note wryly that Momus' traditional Thursday evening parade spot has now been filled by the Knights of Chaos who look and feel much like Momus and who depart from Momus' former den. (In 2006 Chaos borrowed from Momus' "Hades" theme, this time with Katrina as the culprit.)

Proteus was the last of the old-line krewes to stop parading because of the discrimination ordinance, waiting a year to do so, and the first to return by name as it did in 2000. Now it shares its Lundi Gras parade slot with the behemoth Orpheus parade giving Carnival one of its best double headers. Proteus is the surviving link to the grand 19th century night parades.

Zulu as always is different. Its parade is more of a confederacy than a krewe. Different groups, including many containing whites, are able to participate by in effect renting a float, but nevertheless conforming to the character of the parade.

Not at all affected by the discrimination ordinance crisis of 1992, Zulu faced it own race related controversy three decades earlier as reported in the organization's history:

"In the 1960s during the height of black awareness, it was unpopular to be a Zulu. Dressing in a grass skirt and donning a black face were seen as being demeaning. Large numbers of black organizations protested against the Zulu organization, and its membership dwindled to approximately sixteen men. James Russell, a longtime member, served as president in this period, and is credited with holding the organization together and slowly bringing Zulu back to the forefront."

Time and common sense resolved those issues. The decade ended on a more positive note when, in 1968, Zulu began marching on St. Charles and Canal Streets, the route of the other parades. Zulu's previous path along the "back streets" was partially determined because of segregation but also due to necessity. In the early days neighborhood bars along the then route sponsored various floats. (Signs were posted at the bars saying "Zulus will stop here!") After riders dismounted from their floats and entered their sponsoring bar for a bit of revelry, it was difficult to assemble them again. That forced other floats to take off in different directions in pursuit of their obligations. The Zulu parade had become a disjointed affair. Away from the back streets, Zulu could now be seen by a larger audience.

Zulu's greatest crisis came in 2005, the year of Katrina. Its North Broad Street headquarters building was badly damaged. Many parading organizations were hurt by the hurricane but few as badly as Zulu. The group persisted though, and, despite some internal resistance, was committed to parading on 2006. That decision was of historic importance. Beginning with comments made by Mayor Ray Nagin to a group of displaced New Orleanians in Atlanta, there was some sentiment that Carnival parades should not be held in 2006 in the wake of so much disaster. Had Zulu not insisted on parading, Carnival might have been vulnerable to criticisms that white people were parading while blacks suffered. Zulu's resolve, however, showed that the spirit crossed color lines. Nagin would later reverse himself. The parades were held. Mardi Gras that year was not only an artistic success but it provided that first signal to the world that New Orleans was making a comeback. In its own innocent way, Zulu may have saved Carnival.

After the formative period, here are some of the key years in the evolution of the New Orleans Carnival:

1890—Jefferson City Buzzards form. The group, which still marches along the St. Charles parade route on Mardi Gras, is Carnival's oldest marching club.

1893—Proteus introduces the Carnival ball practice of krewe members issuing a "call-out" to women they wish to dance with.

1910—First reported reference of a Zulu coconut being tossed in a parade. This becomes one of the enduring symbols of the New Orleans Carnival. The coconuts were still "hairy" and would not be decorated for several more years.

1924—Krewe of Carrollton founded. The first parade was the product of two neighborhood organizations staging a parade titled, "The Carrollton Carnival."

1930—Municipal Auditorium opens. It is the first public building constructed with the Carnival balls in mind. Its two stages allow for simultaneous pageants, its wide floor encourages grand processions. Elves of Oberon stages the first ball there, February 24, 1930. Queen is Anita M. Nolan.

1931—Perry Young's classic, and somewhat poetic, study of the early Carnival, *The Mistick Krewe: Chronicles of Comus and His Kin* is published.

1933—Alla rises. Combining the words Algiers and Louisiana, the new group gives the West Bank its first lasting major parade.

Mid-City, a krewe intended to bring a parade to the neighborhood it is named after begins parading. The krewe would be a pioneer in animation and would be known for its brilliant foil designs. Despite its name, the krewe would eventually move to the St. Charles route where it would close out the pre-Bacchus parading on the Sunday afternoon before Mardi Gras.

1935—Elks Orleanians presents the first organized truck parade. Rolling on Mardi Gras after the main parades, similar truck parades would follow over the years: Crescent City (1947), the Krewe of Jefferson and Elks Jeffersonian.

1937—Expanding the Carnival weekend by solidifying the Friday night before Mardi Gras, the Hermes parade is founded. The group would be the first to use neon lighting.

1939—Headed by King Sargon, the Knights of Babylon began their reign. Like Hermes, the group stages a traditional parade not linked to old-line membership.

1940S—Mardi Gras Indians end an early history of fighting among tribes and begin putting the emphasis on dances, chants and elaborate costumes. The Carnival Day route of the Indians remains within primarily black neighborhoods.

1944—First Washington, D.C. Carnival ball staged by

Louisianians is held. New Orleans Congressman F. Edward Hebert serves as the ball's first King, though by default, after the original choice, Lt. Col. Leonce Legendre fell ill. Hebert was chosen partially because he was best able to fill Legendre's costume. Ball would grow into a major party-filled, people-watching, politically potent annual event.

1947—Known for its serpentine uptown parade route designed to pass by institutions housing the infirmed and shut-ins, Thoth makes its first march. The parade has become a major presence on the Sunday afternoon before Mardi Gras.

1949—Louis Armstrong presides as King of the Zulu parade. Reign gets national media attention.

With the intent of bringing a parade to the St. Claude Avenue area, the Krewe of Okeanos was founded. The group would eventually move to the Canal Street route and then to St. Charles Avenue.

1950—Former British King Edward VIII and his wife, by then the Duke and Duchess of Windsor, attend the Rex ball. Society watchers are impressed that the Windsors bow to Carnival's monarchs.

1953—Grela, a name created for its home base, Gretna, Louisiana, is formed.

1958—Krewe of Zeus stages its first march. Jefferson Parish's oldest parade was also the first suburban krewe to parade at night.

1959—After many years of presenting balls, Iris takes to the street. The organization is the oldest and largest all female parading group.

1960—Rex introduces the doubloon as a throw, the idea of craftsman H. Alvin Sharpe. The krewe-themed coin would be introduced by other krewes and become the rage for several years until interest waned due to over-saturation.

1966—Featuring its famous winged horse, the Krewe of Pegasus stages its first parade.

1968—Zulu moves to the traditional St. Charles Avenue route exposing the parade to a much larger crowd.

1969—Debut of the Krewe of Bacchus, an organization intended to bring new excitement to Carnival. Bacchus introduced larger floats, a celebrity king and a huge, after the parade indoor extravaganza (originally held at the former Rivergate Convention Center) surrounded by the floats from the parade.

Named after an uptown bar, the Krewe of Tucks emerges as an irreverent parading group.

1971—Carnival got its most creative acronym ever with the creation of the Krewe of NOMTOC which boldly stands for "New Orleans' Most Talked Of Club." The all-black West Bank parade is an outgrowth of the Jugs Social Club.

1972—Cleopatra, the first all-female West Bank parade organization is founded.

1974—Endymion. a previously small Gentilly-based parade (founded in 1967) moves to the Canal Street route and changes into a large scale parade in the spirit of Bacchus. With Endymion marching on the day before Bacchus, the Saturday and Sunday before Mardi Gras are filled with giant parades thereby boosting the tourist market. (Rex Duke a parade critic for *Gambit* newspaper would create the word "Superkrewe" to apply to Bacchus and Endymion then eventually to Orpheus.)

Argus begins parading on Mardi Gras in Jefferson Parish. Though commercialism in parades is banned in neighboring Orleans Parish, Argus would allow sponsorship of its floats.

1975—Krewe of Pontchartrain is founded. Initially it marches in Gentilly then moves to Canal Street before settling on its present St. Charles Avenue route.

1977—Arthur Hardy publishes his first annual *Mardi Gras Guide*.

1979—Strike by New Orleans Police causes the cancellation of all parades in Orleans Parish though some of the city's krewes march in Jefferson Parish that year. The strike, which created a feeling of solidarity between Mayor Ernest "Dutch" Morial and the Carnival organizations, fell apart the day after Mardi Gras.

Jefferson Parish Carnival takes a big leap with the founding of the Krewe of Caesar.

1980—Grateful to see the parades return after the cancellation from the previous year, Mardi Gras enjoyed a new surge of popularity. The decade to follow was a good one for Carnival.

1981—Evolving from a ball-presenting organization, the Krewe of Sparta stages its first procession. Marching on the first Saturday evening of the parade season, the Krewe has been the first major night parade to enliven the St. Charles Avenue route each year

1982—Phunny Phorty Phellows, a re-creation of a 19th century organization, stage their first Twelfth Night streetcar ride. Carrying a sign announcing that "It's Carnival Time," the Phellows become the heralds of Carnival's arrival. The event draws attention to Twelfth Night.

1987—Lundi Gras begins. Rex revives his tradition of arriving by boat on the day before Mardi Gras, this time using Spanish Plaza next to Riverwalk as the staging area. In the early years of Lundi Gras, Proteus made a U-turn at the river end of Poydras to service the crowds watching the Rex arrival. Combined with musical entertainment on the riverfront and, for the first time, fireworks as a part of Carnival, the little-known Creole term "Lundi Gras" (Fat Monday) is applied to the package of events. The phrase catches on and becomes part of the Carnival language.

1992—Controversial civil rights ordinance creates a furor. Comus and Momus stop parading. Proteus does the same a year later but returned in 2000. Tension soothes after passage of compromise ordinance requiring krewes to sign an affidavit declaring their practices are non-discriminatory.

1994—First parade of Orpheus, marching on Lundi Gras evening extends the number of super krewes to three embracing the Saturday, Sunday and then Monday before Mardi Gras. Finer optic lighting was introduced by the krewe's Leviathan float. Of the three "Super Krewes," Orpheus is the only one to have both male and female riders.

1998—LeKrewe D'Etat founded. The all-male satirical krewe is an instant hit and becomes the first satirical group to use fully sculptured float figures to depict satire.

Borrowing from an historic New Orleans Carnival name, the Ancient Druids present their first parade. The group is unique in that it is made up entirely of members from other parade groups who wanted to have an extra chance to ride.

2000—Krewe of Muses founded. The satirical all-female krewe emphasizes diversity and social service.

2001—Suspiciously resembling the old Momus parade, the Knights of Chaos make their debut. Beside having the Momus look, the Knights parade on the Thursday evening before Mardi Gras, a night traditionally known as "Momus Thursday."

2002—First ever bifurcated parade season. Because of the September 11, 2001 tragedy, the Superbowl, which was to be played in New Orleans that year, was delayed a week, coincidentally right in the heart of the parade season. The marching schedule was changed. First week krewes marched the week before Superbowl weekend, the rest marched after. Negotiations with krewe members were tense, but events went smoothly.

2006—Overcoming criticisms that there should be no parade at all soon after Hurricane Katrina, the truncated parade schedule proved instrumental in giving the world its first indication that New Orleans would rebound. Labeled by *New Orleans Magazine* as "the most important Carnival ever" the season was also uplifting for locals.

2007—Though most of the celebrating was done the year before, the year represents the 150th anniversary of the first Comus parade and the continuing parading tradition. Comus set the prototype for all that would follow.

Zeus celebrates its 50th anniversary and therefore the anniversary of the Jefferson Parish Mardi Gras.

2008—Mardi Gras falls on February 5, the earliest date in the history of the organized New Orleans Carnival.

Bacchus celebrates the 40th anniversary of its founding.

Left in its path are oak trees with limbs decorated with beads hanging like icicles. The echo of drums, brass and sirens are in the distance. Vendors push their carts past revelers wearing strings of plastic pearls stacked past their chins. Carnival's march continues— into the future.

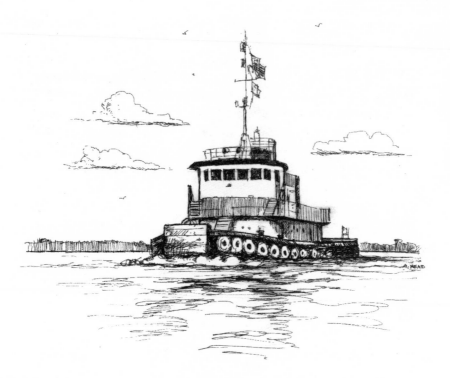

MARCH 3, 1999
AN EXPEDITION IN SEARCH OF
A PLACE NAMED "MARDI GRAS"

This angry, swirling, rock-impeded entrance was the elusive front door of the Mississippi. That stormy night New Orleans history began, in the larger sense, as the Iberville expedition ploughed through gale winds, driving rain and lightening, bumping invisible logs and snags, rocks and sawyers cluttering the Malbouche (Now the North Pass). Exhausted, they camped a short way upstream near the entrance of a bayou.

A SHORT HISTORY OF NEW ORLEANS
BY MEL LEAVITT, LEXICOS PRESS, 1982

THOSE STORMS LIT UP THE SKY along the Mississippi on the evening of March 2, 1699. The party dropped anchor waiting for light of the next day. In one of history's great coincidences, that day, March 3, 1699, happened to be Mardi Gras. As Leavitt reported: "The first place names given Louisiana were, appropriately, Pointe de Mardi Gras and Mardi Gras Bayou."

Three hundred years to the day later, a tugboat, the "Captain Billy Slatten," worked its way up the Mississippi River. An expedition, organized by the Rex organization and including the captains of some of the older Carnival organizations, was on board in search of the bayou and the point.

History could have easily been so different. Had the gales been a bit stronger, the swells a bit more threatening, the party led by French Canadian Pierre Le Moyne Sieur de Iberville might have missed its brush with immortality and would not have been forever linked with the American Carnival. Had the party arrived on Ash Wednesday instead of the day before, the 300th anniversary of their landing may have been ignored by all except the most studious of historians. But because of the coincidence of their arrival, the legacy of the settlers will be forever protected and celebrated within a world of kings and gods.

A Rex flag flew from the tug boat as it worked its way past crew boats and supply ships that service offshore drilling platforms. The fact that those boats were sitting quietly in port spoke loudly about the condition of the offshore oil industry. But the news about the economy, as seen from the Mississippi, was not all-bad. Billy Slatten, the man after whom the boat was named, said that his fleet of 17 tugs, with another on the way, is quite busy directing cargo ships upriver as far as Baton Rouge. For the afternoon though, his line's flagship was a ceremonial barge as it headed toward an outpost known as Fort St. Philip. The structure is one of Plaquemines Parish's twin forts placed there to guard the river from intruders, such as Union Admiral David Farragut, who eventually conquered New Orleans anyway. The other garrison, Fort Jackson, is far better known because it is located on the West Side of the river—the side on which the highway runs. Fort St. Philip, however, is accessible only by boat and not one as big as the tug. Once the "Slatten" got near the fort it stopped and held its position. A small fishing boat ferried passengers from the boat toward the marsh. It leaped across rapids and turned sharply on merging bayous before coming to the fort.

INTO THE MARSH

There who braved the side-trip (and who were willing to sign a waiver against liability for stepping onto this private property) walked through the bramble that lines the old fort. Slatten, who knows the river and its quirks well, believes that the Fort site was Pointe de Mardi Gras because there would have been an inviting sandbar at that location. Unfortunately hardly anything is left of Bayou Mardi Gras. Once again man is the culprit, only this time it is 19th century man. Pierre McGraw, a member of a group called the Monumental Task Committee and who has studied the area, said that the construction of the fort in effect cut off the bayou, which is mostly now a ditch. Slatten pointed to links of the waterways that lace the marsh around the fort as likely having been part of the original stream.

It's hard to imagine a place so desolate as having had so much history. Not only are there the Iberville and Civil War connections, but the infamous period when Plaquemines political boss Leander Perez fortified the place with barbed wire and announced to the national press that he would house civil right demonstrators there if any of them came to Plaquemines Parish. In another era the site was also a hippie compound until their presence became a bit too psychedelic for the local taste.

I was hoping to be able to report that I dug around and found some doubloons dating back to 1699, but that would not be. All that glittered from the shoreline was beer cans, not necessarily popped open there but part of the tidal wash.

On the agenda that day was to dedicate a monument commemorating the 300th anniversary. John Charbonnet, a Rex official, explained that Fort St. Philip was ruled out as the monument's site because, "the only ones who could read it would be the nutria."

CHISELED IN GRANITE

Instead, the tug glided back down river to its dock in Venice. From there the entourage took a bus to the more utilized Fort Jackson. A parish workman hurriedly dug a ditch for a time capsule to be planted there. Meanwhile the delegation gathered on the Fort's top deck for the dedication of a new monument next to where an existing marker tells about the Mardi Gras landing on the other side of the river.

A Rex banner draped the monument until it was ceremonially lifted by reigning Rex Louis Freeman. The words, literally chiseled in granite, told of Rex honoring the occasion of the 300th anniversary. Moved by the moment, Dr. Homer Dupuy, Rex 1963, and so much a Francophile that he once doctored current French President Jacques Chirac when the latter was a young man, spontaneously broke into a chorus of *La Marseillaise*. The French Counsel General at his side joined in. The point was made that the song would not have existed in 1699, but since nobody could hum what Iberville and his group might have sung, it would do.

All of this was done under a cloudless blue sky with just enough of a chill to be delightful. Curiously, during the night before, March 2, a ferocious storm front had raced across the area. Anyone traveling the river as the front struck would have "ploughed through gale winds, driving rain and lightning" just like Iberville's party three centuries ago that night. Carnival remains blessed by its great coincidences.

MARCH 1999

ILLUSTRATION BY ARTHUR NEAD

HOW THE LOUISIANA PURCHASE CHANGED MARDI GRAS

WERE IT NOT FOR the Louisiana Purchase in 1803, Mardi Gras would not be celebrated in New Orleans—at least not the way we know it.

We've heard much about the political and economic impact that the sale had on the nation and the world. It also influenced the way that we celebrated.

Prior to the Purchase, New Orleans was primarily a Creole society. The change in ownership introduced American ways to the territory—and that changed everything.

New Orleans became an American town, but with a French accent, and that's what its Carnival became too. The French had brought the phrase "Mardi Gras" and the tradition of celebrating the day before Ash Wednesday to the New World, but their festivities were mostly in the forms of masquerade balls, dances, occasional makeshift parades, lots of drinking and a few brawls. There was nothing enduring; nothing that made the day memorable. Then along came the Americans.

One of life's best tonics is to combine Europeans traditions with American ambition. In 1857 a group of young men took the emptiness of Mardi Gras night and gave to it the Mistick Krewe of Comus. Suddenly Carnival in New Orleans had lights, sound and the beginning of traditions and continuity. The New Orleans style Carnival parade had begun and all else that would follow, from Alla to Zulu, would be shaped by Comus.

Comus' founders were neither French nor native. Three were born in New York State; two were from Kentucky, another came from Pittsburgh. Three of the six had lived in Mobile at some point during their lives. There they saw a fledgling Carnival celebration that, like New Orleans', was French in name but American in creativity. The founder of Mobile's Cowbellians, a group that would be a model for Comus, was from Pennsylvania.

Philadelphia, not Paris, was the city that most influenced the evolution of the American Carnival. In the 1700s Swedes had introduced to Philadelphia the tradition of "mummery"—masquerading. Mummers marched on New Year's Day, as did the original Cowbellians in Mobile. The American experience synthesized the winter parading traditions of many cultures. In New Orleans a new style of celebration would flower under the collective name of Mardi Gras. Carnival became big business in 1872 with the introduction of the first Rex parade. Rex created a lasting, organized day parade for Mardi Gras that complemented Comus' evening march. The arrival of Rex turned Mardi Gras into a holiday and—by the way—a visitor attraction.

Created 15 years after Comus and during the bitter days of Reconstruction, Rex too was founded mostly by Yankees. The Americans, natives of a land born of a revolution against monarchy, had given Carnival its kings.

Without the Louisiana Purchase, Carnival's evolutionary path could not have spread. Because of the Purchase, a bigger nation was taking shape—and so too was a bigger parade calendar.

JANUARY 2003

IMPORTANT JOB:
NO RECOGNITION—NICE WHISTLE

IN THE FINAL HOUR of the 2002 Mardi Gras, a rare but important ritual was enacted—and hardly anyone noticed. The ceremony was also one of Carnival's briefest.

As the Rex Ball was closing—after the king and queen had left their benches, and while most of the audience was either heading home or moving down the hall to the Comus Ball, two men in white ties and tails approached each other from different points on the floor. The men's meeting point was in front of the box seats where both of their wives happened to be. Reaching their destination, the two stopped and stood face to face. Then something happened that caused gasps from those few left in the Municipal Auditorium who happened to be watching. One of the men lifted his whistle cord from around his neck and placed it around the neck of the other. There was applause, a few cheers and lots of expressions of surprise. The Queen of Carnival, who happened to be looking back at the ball floor on her way to meet Comus, seemed tearful, happy and surprised. The man who received the whistle was kin.

For a celebration that thrives on pageantry, one of its most important transitions happens simply. The passing of the whistle signaled a change in the captaincy of the Rex Organization.

Tradition has it that the identity of the Rex Captain is kept secret. The reason for that, as Mark Twain once wrote in explaining the rituals of the local Carnival, is not for fear of the police but for the sake of tradition itself.

In the power structure of New Orleans Carnival, the captains are the bosses of their krewes. While the reign of monarchs lasts just for a day and their duties are strictly ceremonial, captains perform as Prime Ministers concerned with the day to day governance.

While all krewes have captains, the man who wears the whistle for Rex historically takes on an extra level of importance in the guidance of the entire Carnival. "It is the best civic job there is," the outgoing captain used to say about the position he held for nearly nine years. If so, it is NOT because of the political or business gain that comes with the title. Secret jobs are hardly marketable for career advancement. Besides, the men who become captain have usually already found their place in the corporate world. Other than getting to ride a white horse and being invited to lots of debutante parties, there are few perks that come with the job. But for those who like to mix it up with everyday issues and controversies, atop the white horse is the place to be. Whenever Carnival has had crises, Rex's captains have usually been up front facing them. In 1979 when a police strike caused all parades in New Orleans to be cancelled, the Rex captain of that time stood alongside Mayor Dutch Morial in defying the police union. During the discrimination ordinance controversy of 1991–92, a different Rex Captain stood courageously in front of the New Orleans City Council taking the heat from both sides: some fellow captains who thought he was being too accommodating versus the ordinance's proponents who thought he was not being accommodating enough. The Captain also worked behind the scenes. When the full story is known, it will show that the relatively peaceful resolution of the crisis was due largely to legal problem solving initiated by Rex leadership.

Rex's most recent Captain served as chairman of the city's Mardi Gras Coordinating Committee having to deal with issues from the mundane—float fire extinguisher specifications to the critical—Carnival safety hazards.

Founded in 1872, the Rex Organization's first captain was a newspaperman with a flair for the literary named E.C. Hancock. Even in its founding Rex was solving a problem by creating a day parade around which miscellaneous street maskers could be organized. By claiming the title of King of Carnival, the group also created a populist monarch. The fact that the new parade would be good for tourism during those tense years of Reconstruction when people were nervous about traveling was probably not lost on organizers.

As Carnival grew and other krewes were founded, Rex, by the mid-twentieth century, had fallen in the shadows—still parading but without much sparkle. By the early 1960s, however, the Rex revival was in place under the leadership of the late Darwin Fenner who is credited with rebuilding the organization. (Protocol allows for captains to be identified once they are deceased; understandably the four living former captains are in no hurry to be identified.)

In the age of the super krewe, Rex is neither the biggest nor the richest of the parading organizations, but it is the group with the best grasp of Carnival's traditions, style and elegance. As the holders of the title, "King of Carnival," Rex takes its civic responsibilities seriously.

I have never been one to justify Carnival's significance just in terms of economic impact—the season also creates community spirit and provides an urban identity. When Mardi Gras is measured in terms of tourism dollars, however, those who are its leaders are as civically important as the forces behind the New Orleans Jazz & Heritage

Festival and the Convention Center, only the Carnival guys wear a mask.

One also wears a whistle. When thunder is heard during Carnival sometimes it's from gathering storm clouds or sometimes it is just approaching drums. While others revel, the man on the white horse has to be ready to respond to either situation.

DECEMBER, 2003

CARNIVAL DURING TIMES OF UNREST

BY EARLY JANUARY, 1973, that year's Carnival celebration seemed to be in deep trouble. The town was on edge. One newspaper columnist suggested that the city might consider canceling the parades. More locals than usual were talking about leaving town for Mardi Gras, not necessarily for a skiing trip, but as a safety precaution.

Carnival season that year had begun with an ominous start. On the day after Twelfth Night, January 7, 1973, a sniper hiding atop a hotel held a city in siege. He killed seven people before coming to a dramatic end as he was blasted by machine gunfire from a circling helicopter. Time would prove that the sniper acted alone, but during a decade that had included the assassinations of John Kennedy, Martin Luther King and Robert Kennedy as well as the civil unrest triggered by the Viet Nam war, the nation was jittery. New Orleanians, having now seen the smoke in their skyline, knew fear firsthand.

Nevertheless, the celebration continued. The date of Mardi Gras was late that year, March 6, allowing some time for healing though the first parades were less than six weeks after the incident. Surprisingly Carnival proved to be part of the healing process. Howard Mahorner as Rex and Bob Hope as Bacchus, reined over a city seemingly determined to stage a peaceful, cheery Carnival. Hope even brought an entourage with him that required 45 hotel rooms. He used the occasion to tape an edition of "The Bob Hope Show" on location. An estimated audience of 50 million saw the comedian ruling over a festive city. There was no evidence of the sorrow that the town had recently suffered.

Carnival, when it needs to be justified, is most often defended in terms of economic impact. While the dollar figures are impressive, we maintain that the season is also good for the soul, and many times that has proven to be priceless. Carnival brings to the streets thousands of people competing against each other at bead snatching, yet peacefully co-existing. The ritual has helped us renew beliefs in ourselves as a community. It did so in 1973. It did so through the years when New Orleans had the highest murder rate in the nation. And it did so last year when our Carnival was the first major festival in the nation celebrated after the September 11 tragedy.

In the years since '72, the New Orleans Carnival has occasionally faced its own internal strife: a police strike in '79 prohibited any parades from marching in the city; a civil rights ordinance controversy in 1992 caused some krewes to drop out and triggered bitter feelings. Yet, Carnival today is bigger and probably stronger than ever. Like the city it serves, Carnival always seems to be so vulnerable yet astounds with its resilience.

A Carnival such as ours could not exist in many other cities and could never be started new anywhere. Ours is an evolutionary product of cultures and traditions given life by generally favorable winter weather. Because New Orleans celebrates Carnival, there is rhythm vibrating in the streets and there are beads dangling from trees. We worry about the distant thunder, but maybe it is only the beat of approaching drums.

JANUARY 2003

ILLUSTRATION BY ARTHUR NEAD

ENDYMION AND THE BACCHUS INFLUENCE

ANNIVERSARY DATES for the Krewe of Endymion are like Mexican Independence days—there are options from which to choose. Just as the Mexicans can celebrate independence from Spain and independence from France (plus revolutions against an occasional dictator), Endymion had two births. The first was in 1966 when the group was founded (or should it be '67 when it first paraded), and the second was in 1974 when it was born again. That was the year the organization blasted to the top of the Carnival scene after changing from a routine, little-noticed Gentilly based parade to a mega-krewe that is now the largest in all of Carnival.

Whichever way the numbers are counted, the quantifiable fact is that 1996 marked the 30th time that a parade called Endymion is on the schedule. That's reason enough to declare an anniversary. Happy 30th, Endymion.

By the early '70s, when Endymion was between lives, Carnival was experiencing its own revolution. The Krewe of Bacchus, which first paraded in 1969, had shaken things up, bringing to the streets a grander, more visual Carnival parade than had ever been seen. The floats were bigger than ever; the themes were designed for mass appeal. It was a parade for the MTV generation before MTV existed. Bacchus broke from conventional ways: the role of Bacchus would be played by a different celebrity each year. Instead of a society ball the krewe rolled its entire parade into the Rivergate Convention Center where a dinner dance bash was held. There was a feeling of newness and excitement about this krewe.

Bacchus' influence was so enormous that practically every fledgling krewe at the time promised to be "like Bacchus." None succeeded, except Endymion, which not only became like Bacchus but went on to establish a character of its own.

Endymion is the only krewe to have more than a thousand members. (Not counting organizations which are really a confederation of many groups, such as the truck parades in New Orleans and the samba pageants in Rio, Endymion is, quite probably, the biggest Carnival parade club in the world.) Bacchus does not have a Queen, Endymion does and the Endymion king is not a celebrity but a krewe member. The krewe's fans do see stars though; they are scattered throughout the parade (one year including Donna Summer and KC & the Sunshine Band). The celebs hitch a ride in the procession to perform at Endymion's party that evening.

Endymion introduced the succession of mini-floats carrying feathery bedecked maids and dukes—an innovation that other krewes have tried to imitate, often as a substitute for real floats, with far less success. For Endymion the mini-floats are just a prelude to the larger segment of the parade to follow. Endymion has become a master of prelude, so much prelude that one year the lapsed time, with only occasional brief stops, between the arrival of the lead police unit and the king's float was one hour. This is a multi-beer run parade.

For most organizations the captain is an obscure figure whose identity, by tradition, is kept secret. There is no such tradition with this group. Few parades are as identified with one person as Endymion is linked to its captain and founder, Ed Muniz. A radio station owner by trade, he is the only person who rules in two different parishes with two different titles: one civil, one royal. He was elected Mayor of Kenner in 2006 and he is a New Orleans parade captain. For one night a year he lords over the city most often while having a stand-in wearing the plumage-laden captain's outfit with its top-heavy feathery crown. That allows the real captain to ride in a lead unit, less bedecked but more capable of being in control of the action.

Muniz is part of a genre of guys who were raised with New Orleans' culture and tradition but who later moved to the suburbs yet who have tried to embellish the city's influences. Near where the Endymion parade turns on to Canal Street is the Centanni home, once decorated annually with a display of Christmas lights and displays. Little Al Copeland was among the city's kids who would each year gawk at the decorations. He resolved to do that himself one day. Muniz remembered the Carnival parades of his youth and wanted to bring something bigger and better to the city.

What he has brought is more than a parade but a street festival. As someone who lives near the Endymion Canal Street route I can attest that "Endymion Saturday" is like no other day of the year. The entire neighborhood is landlocked by traffic and barricaded streets as early as 3 p.m. leaving those of us who are entrapped with little else to do but to party. For a few hours of one day a year old city streets are like what they used to be before air conditioners and television when people walked those streets and mingled easily. Some neighbors who are only seen once a year appear on Endymion Saturday.

I hope for the best for Endymion. I also hope that no krewe ever tries to be like Endymion. That would requires more additional energy and people power than the city can handle. Besides, there is still so much of Endymion to behold. At its best the parade is like a really intricate movie with so many scenes and sub-plots that it needs to be seen several times to absorb. Last year Endymion introduced, without the fanfare that it deserved, a new permanent float to its collection. Built as a tandem, so that it can turn corners, the float is entitled "Welcome to the New Orleans Mardi Gras." It is a marvelous addition that is visually busy and that carries 150 riders. The new float is the largest in all of Carnival. Some entire krewes do not have as many members as the number who ride on that one float.

Endymion is named after a shepherd boy who was a mythological symbol of youth. At 30 the krewe maintains its youthful ambition. It does so because there was once a boy in Gentilly whose dream was Olympian in size. That's all the more reason to lift a goblet, perhaps filled by the wine god Bacchus.

FEBRUARY 1996

POPE'S PHARMACY

LOOKING FOR LANDMARKS—
CARNIVAL'S TOP TEN

AS INVITATIONS GO, it was brief and to the point. But what an impact it would have. In early January 1857 a small group of New Orleans men received the following message:

"You are requested to meet a few of your friends at the Club room over the Gem, on Royal Street, on Saturday, 10th, at 7 o'clock."

From that meeting, and a subsequent gathering held on February 8, came an organization that would forever affect the city's reputation, character, traditions and economy—all for the better. The new group would be called "The Mistick Krewe of Comus."

Carnival as it would become known was created in the room above the Gem Cafe on the 100 block of Royal. Prior to Comus, Mardi Gras was celebrated in New Orleans, but in no way that lasted. There were miscellaneous makeshift parades, lots of disorganized street rabble and a few decent soirees and balls. Comus gave the season a lasting presence. It created the New Orleans style of parade and established many traditions. From then on, wherever the season was celebrated in North America, it was in imitation of New Orleans. In terms of the length of celebration and the multitude of events, the local Carnival would become the largest in the world.

By any standards, the Gem should be a revered historic landmark, but it is not. The building still exists, housing, on the first floor, a curio shop and a convenience store. The Carnival Establishment should have embraced the building decades ago, but it never happened. In 2001 Arthur Hardy, publisher of the *Mardi Gras Guide*, arranged to have a plaque placed there commemorating the birthplace of the modern Carnival. Finally, a first step toward preserving the sites of Carnival's heritage.

There are other important sites worth remembering. Here's my list of the top tens.

1.) *The Gem Cafe—127 Royal Street.* For all the reasons mentioned above.

2.) *Pope's Pharmacy—Prytania and Jackson Avenue. (Uptown riverside corner.)* If the Gem was the birthplace of the modern Carnival, Pope's Pharmacy was where it was conceived. It was there in late 1856 that six men met, discussed the idea and decided to have the meeting at the Gem. The proprietor, Dr. J. H. Pope would be the one to suggest the name,"The Mistick Krewe of Comus." The building still stands and, appropriately, is owned by someone who has been very active in Carnival.

3.) *St. Charles Hotel—200 block of St. Charles Avenue.* Now the site of what is commonly known as Place St. Charles, the hotel was where the meetings were held from which Rex evolved. In 19th century New Orleans, it was the hub of activity and the place where many important visitors stayed. Only three blocks away from where Comus was born, Rex came to life here.

4.) *Corner of Magazine and Julia Streets.* There should be an historic marker here. At 9 p.m. on Mardi Gras evening 1857 the first Comus Parade began at this spot. Music and lights stirred the stillness in what is now commonly referred to as the Warehouse District. Carnival got its glow that night.

5.) *Pickwick Club—115 St. Charles Avenue.* First there was the parade, then there was the men's club around which it would center. When Comus paraded, the club's balcony was the reviewing stand for the Queen and her court that would be toasted there by Comus. Arrival at the Pickwick Club also meant that the Comus Parade was about to make its turn onto Canal Street en route to the Auditorium bringing Carnival to a close.

6.) *Boston Club—824 Canal Street.* Though there is no formal relationship between this club and the Rex organization, for many years it was the epicenter of Rex activity. The building, which until 1992 was also the place where the Queen of Carnival and her court would review the Parade, is one of the most elegant along Canal Street.

7.) *Gallier Hall—546 St. Charles Avenue.* More than a former City Hall, the building has been Carnival's ceremonial capitol. In 1872 it was where the visiting Grand Duke Alexis watched the first Rex parade. Whether a parade's main route is Canal Street or St. Charles, all make the turn to stop at Gallier Hall to be toasted by the Mayor or a Council member. In the early 1960's once the current City Hall was completed, parades changed their routes to stop there instead. After a couple of year, however, they missed the old place. Gallier Hall has been a part of the parades path ever since.

8.) *Municipal Auditorium—Orleans Avenue at N. Rampart Street.* There have been many places where Carnival balls have been held, but the Auditorium is the only building ever designed with the balls in mind. Its spaciousness allowed for grand marches, its back rooms provided a huge dressing space and party areas for the guys in the krewe. When the building was used as a temporary casino and for several years after Hurricane Katrina, the krewes had to go elsewhere. There was concern they would never return, but most have. Truth is, there's no place better.

9.) *1100 Perdido Street. Tramps club room.* From that setting (no longer standing) the Zulu organization would emerge,

10.) *Brennan's Restaurant—417 Royal Street.* Now for something different, and a bit more contemporary. It was here that the meeting were held in 1968 leading to the formation of the Bacchus organization. As the first of the Super-krewes. Bacchus added a new dimension to Carnival, expanded the activity and made the weekend before Mardi Gras as big as the day itself in terms of crowd size. Somewhere between the entree and the Bananas Foster, Carnival took a huge leap into the future.

May that future create many more landmarks.

FEBRUARY 2001